DATE DUE

31472
Vernonia School District v.
Acton: Drug Testing in
Deborah A. Persico
AR B.L.: 9.6
Points: 4.0

Vernonia School District v. Acton

This book is dedicated to Mary Luscia Gem.

Vernonia School District v. Acton

Drug Testing in Schools

Deborah A. Persico

Landmark Supreme Court Cases

Enslow Publishers, Inc.

40 Industrial Road   PO Box 38
Box 398   Aldershot
Berkeley Heights, NJ 07922   Hants GU12 6BP
USA   UK

http://www.enslow.com

Library of Congress Cataloging-in-Publication Data

Persico, Deborah A.
　　Vernonia School District v. Acton: drug testing in schools/
Deborah A. Persico.
　　　　p.　cm.
　　Includes bibliographical references and index.
　　Summary: Describes the 1995 Supreme Court case which held that
public school officials could do mandatory drug testing if they showed
that a drug problem existed among the students, even though individual
students were not suspected.
　　ISBN 0-7660-1087-2
　　1. Vernonia School District 47J (Or.)—Trials, litigation, etc.—Juvenile
literature.　2. Acton, James—Trials, litigation, etc.—Juvenile literature.
3. Students—Drug testing—Oregon—Juvenile literature.　4. Athletes—Drug
testing—Oregon—Juvenile literature.　5. Drug testing—Law and legislation
—Oregon—Juvenile literature.　6. Searches and seizures—United States—
Juvenile literature. [1. Vernonia School District 47J (Or.)—Trials, litigation, etc.
2. Acton, James—Trials, litigation, etc.　3. Drug testing—Law and legislation.
4. Searches and seizures.]　I. Title.　II. Title: Vernonia School　District versus Acton.
KF228　V47P47　1999
344.73'0793—dc21　　　　　　　　　　　　　　98-48872
　　　　　　　　　　　　　　　　　　　　　　　　　CIP
　　　　　　　　　　　　　　　　　　　　　　　　　AC

Printed in the United States of America

10 9 8 7 6 5 4 3 2 1

To Our Readers:
All Internet addresses in this book were active and appropriate when we
went to press. Any comments or suggestions can be sent by e-mail to
Comments@enslow.com or to the address on the back cover.

Photo Credits: Courtesy of Timothy R. Volpert, p. 63; Courtesy of Thomas M.
Christ, p. 13; Courtesy of *The Star Ledger*, pp. 47, 70; Corel Corporation, p. 82;
Dane Peland photographer, Courtesy of the United States Supreme Court, p. 92;
National Archives, pp. 18, 31; Reproduced from the collections of the Library of
Congress, pp. 25, 45, 86, 89, 101, 113.

Cover Photo: The Stock Market/Ted Horowitz

Contents

Acknowledgments

The author would like to offer special thanks to Thomas M. Christ, Esquire, for his special insight into the Actons' case; Timothy R. Volpert, Esquire, for his special insight into Vernonia School District's case; Joseph Virgilio, my husband and best friend; Lena and Ralph Persico, my parents; and Dorothy Flaherty, my neighbor and friend.

1

The School District's Drug Testing Policy

In the fall of 1991 James Acton was a seventh grader at Washington Grade School in Vernonia, Oregon. Vernonia is a small logging town with only about three thousand residents. The Vernonia School District has one high school and three elementary schools. There are no fast-food restaurants or teen centers in town. Sports play a big part in the lives of most of Vernonia's high school and elementary school students. James Acton played basketball and ran track at his school, and he decided to try out for football in the fall of 1991.

Shortly before football tryouts, Acton had a physical examination at the Vernonia Health Clinic. As part of that exam, he gave a urine sample for drug testing. At the first Washington Grade School football practice, though, each team member was handed a drug testing consent form. The student athlete was told that he and his parents had to consent to the school conducting random drug testing of athletes. If either the student or his parents did not sign the form, the student would not be allowed to participate in school sports.

The Drug Test

The Vernonia School District had a "Student Athlete Drug Policy" that required random drug testing for anyone who wanted to participate in school athletics. The reason for the drug policy was "to create a safe, drug free, environment for student athletes and assist them in getting help when needed."[1] Athletes would first be tested at the beginning of the season. Then, once each week, a student supervised by two adults drew the names of 10 percent of the athletes for random testing. If a student was taking prescription medication, however, he or she had to provide the school with a copy of the prescription or a note from a doctor, because certain medications could have an effect on the test results.

If a student was selected for random testing, he or she had to give a urine sample. That meant that the student would go into an empty locker room with an adult monitor. Each boy selected had to produce a urine sample at a urinal. He was fully clothed and his back was to a male monitor. The monitor had to stand about fifteen feet away. Each girl selected produced a urine sample from inside a closed stall. The female monitor could hear her but could not see her. The girl or boy would then give the sample to the monitor, who would send it to a laboratory to test for amphetamines, cocaine, and marijuana. The laboratory results were 99.94 percent accurate.

The laboratory did not know the name of the student who gave the urine sample. Each student was given an identification number to place on a form sent to the lab with the sample. When the lab completed its testing, it mailed test results to the superintendent of schools for the Vernonia School District. The superintendent then contacted the principal, vice principal, or athletic director at the school where a student had been tested. No other person was allowed to see the results.

If the urine sample tested positive for drugs, meaning that it showed signs that the student athlete was using drugs, the school policy required the student to give a second urine sample. If the second test was negative, that was the end of the testing; the student was allowed to participate in sports. If the second test was positive, though, the school called a meeting with the student's parents.

The school policy gave the student athlete who had tested positive for drug use two choices. The athlete could choose to participate in a six-week-long drug assistance program that included weekly urine tests. If this option was chosen, the athlete could still play sports. If the athlete did not want to participate in the drug program, he or she would be suspended from all sports for the remainder of the season and for the next two seasons.

The school policy also required that a student be automatically suspended from sports if he or she tested positive a second time. If the athlete tested positive a third time, he or she would be suspended from all athletics for the remainder of the current season and for the next two seasons.

The Consent Form

James Acton took the consent form home to his parents.

The form provided spaces for the student's signature and the signatures of his or her parents.

Wayne and Judy Acton discussed the form and the school's policy with their son over the weekend. The three decided not to sign the form because they felt that the

Drug Testing Consent Form

I understand fully that my performance as a participant and the reputation of my school are dependent, in part, on my conduct as an individual. I hereby agree to accept and abide by the standards, rules, and regulations set forth by Vernonia School District Board and the sponsors for the activity in which I participate.

I also authorize the Vernonia School District to conduct a test on a urine specimen which I provide to test for drugs and/or alcohol use. I also authorize the release of information concerning the results of such a test to the Vernonia School District and to the parents and/or guardians of the student.

This shall be deemed a consent pursuant to the Family Education Right to Privacy Act for the release of the above information to the parties named above.[2]

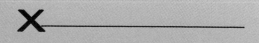

The form that James Acton was required to sign in order to participate in school athletics was worded this way.

mandatory drug testing violated James's constitutional right to privacy. James Acton and his parents scheduled a meeting with Randy Aultman, the principal of Washington Grade School.

At the meeting the Acton family explained that they objected to the drug testing policy of the Vernonia School District because it required James to submit to a drug test, even though the school had no reason to believe that James used drugs. Principal Aultman told the Actons that James could not participate in athletics unless all three of them signed the consent form. The Actons complained to the district superintendent, Ellis Mason, but he, too, told them they had to sign the form if James wanted to play sports. The Actons refused to sign the form, and the school refused to allow James to participate in any school sports.

The Actons File a Lawsuit

The Actons did not give up. Wayne and Judy Acton called the American Civil Liberties Union (ACLU), a group known for handling cases involving civil rights. The ACLU agreed to file a lawsuit against the Vernonia School District on behalf of the Actons. The ACLU assigned attorney Thomas M. Christ to the case.

Because James was a minor, he could not file a lawsuit in his own name. Mr. Christ filed the suit naming

The American Civil Liberties Union (ACLU) agreed to file a lawsuit against the Vernonia School District on behalf of the Actons. Thomas M. Christ (right, with his arm around James Acton) was assigned to the case.

Wayne and Judy Acton as plaintiffs, on behalf of James. He filed the complaint in the federal trial court, called the United States District Court for the District of Oregon. The complaint asked the court to find that the school district's drug testing policy was unlawful. It also asked the court to enjoin, or stop, the district from enforcing the policy and from interfering with James's participation in school athletic programs.

How would the Vernonia School District respond to the Actons' complaint? How would the federal court decide the case? The United States Supreme Court would eventually become interested in James's case— but why? How would the Supreme Court's decision affect the rights of students in schools around the country? Before we can answer these questions, we need to travel back through history to see how James Acton's case developed.

2

The History of Search and Seizure Law

The original thirteen colonies expressed anger toward Britain's domination years before the American Revolution. In 1772 Samuel Adams helped compile the "Rights of the Colonists and a List of Infringements and Violations of Rights."[1] In this document he voiced the concerns of many future revolutionaries. In particular, Adams disapproved of Britain's use of the general warrant, a document that allowed British officers to break down the door of a person's home at any time to conduct a search and to seize any goods they thought were evidence of a crime. Adams wrote:

> Thus, our houses and even our bedchambers are exposed to be ransacked, our boxes, chests and trunks

broke open ravaged and plundered by wretches whom no prudent man would venture to employ even as menial servants. . . . Those Officers may under colour of law and the cloak of a general warrant break thro' the sacred rights of the Domicil, ransack mens houses . . . and with little danger to themselves commit the most horrid murders.[2]

Developing the Bill of Rights

It was this anger that led the colonies to declare the general warrant illegal in 1776. The Virginia Declaration of Rights was adopted on June 12, 1776, and it was followed by similar declarations in Maryland, Pennsylvania, North Carolina, and Massachusetts. It was clear that the colonists would no longer tolerate general warrants.

This philosophy surfaced again in 1789, when the newly formed federation, free of British rule, drafted its own Constitution. When this document was submitted for approval to the Constitutional Convention on September 17, 1787, it did not include the Bill of Rights. Virginian James Madison, a member of the House of Representatives, looked to the individual state constitutions for guidance in developing the Bill of Rights. In addition to the various rights, he also wanted to include a provision about warrants. The proposal Madison submitted is almost identical to the following words, which we now know as the Fourth Amendment to the Constitution of the United States:

> The right of the people to be secure in their persons, houses, papers, and effects, against unreasonable searches and seizures, shall not be violated; and no Warrants shall issue, but upon probable cause, supported by Oath or affirmation, and particularly describing the place to be searched, and the persons or things to be seized.[3]

Fourth Amendment Guarantees

Although the amendment clearly guaranteed privacy and security to all citizens, the specific language used in the amendment would lend itself to a multitude of interpretations for many years to come. What is search and seizure? What is unreasonable search and seizure? What did the drafters mean by the term *probable cause*? When does a person have a legitimate expectation of privacy in his or her personal property? Who is subject to the restrictions of the Fourth Amendment? What is the remedy for a violation of the Fourth Amendment?

What Is Search and Seizure?

In 1886 the United States Supreme Court had an opportunity to answer the first question—"What is search and seizure?" In *Boyd* v. *United States* (1886) the federal government argued that a court order in a civil case requiring a defendant to turn over his private

Virginian James Madison, a member of the House of Representatives in 1789, looked to the individual state constitutions for guidance on developing the Bill of Rights.

accounting books, invoices, and records did not amount to a "search and seizure" under the Fourth Amendment. This was because the federal agents did not forcibly enter the defendant's home to search for his papers.[4] The Supreme Court did not agree that the Fourth Amendment is triggered only where there is "forcible entry." It held that the court order amounted to a search and seizure. It also held that an order requiring a person to turn over evidence that may be incriminating also violates that defendant's privilege against self-incrimination, which is provided for in the Fifth Amendment.

Twenty-eight years after *Boyd*, in 1914, the Supreme Court continued to develop its interpretation of the Fourth Amendment. It heard arguments in the case of *Weeks* v. *United States*.[5] A federal marshal had entered the home of Fremont Weeks without a search warrant and confiscated his personal papers. The trial court had allowed the prosecutor, that is, the attorney for the government, to use that evidence against Weeks to convict him of a federal offense. Fremont Weeks appealed his case all the way to the Supreme Court.

Cases at the State Level

The long road Fremont Weeks traveled to the Supreme Court in 1914 is basically the same road criminal defendants must travel today. Generally, if a defendant believes evidence has been seized in violation of Fourth Amendment rights, he or she files with the trial court a document known as a motion to suppress evidence. If the trial court allows the government to use that evidence at trial and the defendant is convicted, that is, found guilty of the crime, the defendant can ask a higher court, usually called a court of appeals, to review his or her case. If the court of appeals agrees with the defendant, it will reverse the conviction. That means it will strike the defendant's conviction from the record and order the trial court to conduct a new trial without allowing the use of the improperly seized evidence. In many instances, because of the crucial nature of some evidence, a prosecutor will then decline to prosecute. There is no longer any evidence to support a conviction.

If the court of appeals disagrees with the defendant in a state case, the defendant can appeal to a state court of last resort, usually called a state supreme court. If that court upholds the conviction, the defendant may then seek review by the United States Supreme Court.

Cases at the Federal Level

On the other hand, if the defendant was convicted in a federal district court, which is the trial court level of the

United States court system, the first appeal is to a federal circuit court of appeals. Then the defendant can seek review by the United States Supreme Court.

Fremont Weeks's case started in a federal district court and ended up in the United States Supreme Court. The Supreme Court agreed with Weeks. It ruled that because federal agents searched Weeks's home without a warrant, the search was clearly unreasonable under the Fourth Amendment and the evidence should have been suppressed. To suppress evidence means that the court excludes its use at trial. Suppressing evidence in this way is commonly known as invoking the exclusionary rule.

Did the *Weeks* decision mean that law enforcement officers would *always* need a warrant before they could search? The answer, as you will see, is no.

Probable Cause and Searches

Courts generally begin with the theory that any search or seizure of evidence that violates a person's personal security is *per se*, in and of itself, unreasonable. This theory generally holds true unless a court issues a warrant based on probable cause.[6] But, not surprisingly, there are many exceptions to the general rule. The first exception is that in some circumstances the law enforcement officer can justify a warrantless search if there is probable cause to conduct a search.

What did the drafters of the Fourth Amendment mean by the term *probable cause?* In the 1925 case *Carroll* v. *United States,* the United States Supreme Court defined *probable cause.* The Court found that probable cause exists where "the facts and circumstances within [the officials'] knowledge and of which they had reasonably trustworthy information [are] sufficient in themselves to warrant a man of reasonable caution in the belief" that a crime has occurred and that evidence would be found in a particular place.[7] In other words, if a police officer has trustworthy information showing that a crime has occurred and that evidence of that crime will be found in a certain place, the judge will issue a legal document called a warrant. This document authorizes the officer to search for and seize the items named in the warrant. The person named in the warrant may also be arrested.

Using the term *probable cause,* the *Carroll* case carved out one of the first major exceptions to the warrant requirement. It noted a difference between searching for and seizing evidence concealed in a house or similar place and evidence being transported in a moving vehicle, such as a car, boat, or airplane. Since a vehicle can be quickly moved, the court in the *Carroll* case held that a law enforcement officer may legally search a vehicle without a warrant if there is probable cause to believe a crime has occurred and that the evidence is in the vehicle.

Did the *Carroll* case mean that a police officer *must* have probable cause every time that a search without a warrant was conducted? Again, the answer is no.

Warrantless Searches

The Supreme Court created exceptions to the warrant requirement. However, it also determined that in some cases government agents could justify a warrantless search even if they did not have probable cause. In the landmark case of *Terry* v. *Ohio* in 1968, the Court had to determine whether Mr. Terry's Fourth Amendment rights had been violated when a police officer patted down the outside of his clothing, felt a pistol, and ordered Terry to remove his coat and remove the pistol—all without a warrant.[8]

Nine Justices sit on the Supreme Court, and it uses a democratic system to decide cases—the majority rules. In *Terry*, the majority of the Justices agreed that Terry had been "seized" by the police officer and subjected to a "search" within the meaning of the Fourth Amendment. But did that mean the officer should have had a warrant and probable cause to search?

Cleveland police detective Martin McFadden had testified in court that he had reason to believe that Terry and two others were planning to rob a store. He saw Terry and another man standing together on a street corner for a long time. He watched as they paced along the same route, pausing to stare in the same store window. He then saw them join a third man. Detective McFadden decided to investigate.

Detective McFadden did not have probable cause to believe that Terry had actually committed a crime. Chief Justice Earl Warren recognized, though, that it would have been poor police work for the detective not to investigate. He further wrote on behalf of the Supreme Court that it would be unreasonable to deny police the power to protect themselves from potentially armed and dangerous suspects under these circumstances. Consequently, the Court ruled that, for their own protection, police officers are justified in conducting a search for weapons when they have reasonable grounds to believe that "criminal activity may be afoot" and that persons with whom they are dealing may be armed and dangerous.[9]

The Court had ruled that police officers do not always need probable cause to justify a search or a seizure. The Court then extended the *Terry* v. *Ohio* reasonableness standard to many other types of searches

In *Terry* v. *Ohio* in 1968, Chief Justice Earl Warren (center) wrote the decision on behalf of the Supreme Court. The Court ruled that, for their own protection, police officers are justified in conducting a search for weapons when they have reasonable suspicion of criminal activity.

and seizures. For example, police officers may search a passenger compartment of a car if they have reasonable suspicion of criminal activity.[10] The United States Border Patrol is authorized to stop a vehicle and question its occupants if the agents have reasonable suspicion that the vehicle may contain illegal aliens.[11]

In some instances, the Supreme Court has recognized a need for states to regulate certain activities for the good of the general public. In these cases, the Court has authorized searches and seizures without warrants, probable cause, *or* reasonable suspicion. Government agents can inspect mines and the businesses of gun dealers and alcohol dealers. The United States Coast Guard or United States Customs Service can board a vessel and examine documents. Firefighters can remain in a building to investigate the cause of a fire after it has been extinguished.

Why would the Supreme Court allow so many exceptions? Doesn't the Fourth Amendment *require* both a warrant and probable cause?

Take another look at the language of the Fourth Amendment—"The right of the people to be secure . . . against unreasonable searches and seizures." The Supreme Court has emphasized time and again that the Constitution does not forbid *all* searches and seizures— it forbids only *unreasonable* searches and seizures. The

Court has determined that in many instances, like the ones noted earlier in this chapter, searches and seizures are *reasonable,* even though government agents did not have a warrant or probable cause to believe a crime had been committed.

The Balancing Test

If some searches and seizures require probable cause and some do not, how does the Supreme Court make that determination? Generally, it uses a balancing test. It considers the privacy interests of the individual searched as well as why the government wants to search without a warrant or probable cause. An individual must first show that there is a reasonable "expectation of privacy" in the property searched. For example, placing an object in a container that protects it from view, such as a purse or suitcase, demonstrates an expectation of privacy. The government must show that its reasons for the search—for example, the health, welfare, or safety of the general public—are more important than the individual's personal privacy.

The balancing test that courts use depends for the most part on the particular categories of searches. For example, in car searches the courts balance a car owner's right to privacy against the government's interest in securing evidence that could be easily moved. In searches by health officials, courts balance a business owner's right to privacy against the likelihood that serious public health risks would go undetected.

The preceding examples show that Fourth Amendment issues can be raised in a variety of situations in both federal and state courts. That was not always the case, however.

Fourth Amendment Applying Only to Federal Cases

In early cases the United States Supreme Court had held that the Fourth Amendment applied only to federal cases.[12] Federal crimes include espionage (spying), income tax evasion, destruction of national defense materials, violation of immigration laws, and stowing away on vessels or aircraft. The laws of the nation are enforced by United States attorneys in federal courts.

Due Process and the Fourteenth Amendment

In 1949, in the case of *Wolf* v. *Colorado*, the Supreme Court took a step that would affect thousands of cases to come.[13] It began by discussing the Fourteenth Amendment to the Constitution, adopted in 1868. This amendment prohibits any state from depriving any person ". . . of life, liberty, or property, without due process of law."[14] This is known as the Due Process

Clause of the Fourteenth Amendment. Due process means that before the state can take away a person's life, freedom, or property, that person is entitled to a fair hearing that must follow certain rules of procedure. In a monumental step, the Supreme Court ruled in *Wolf* that the concept of liberty in the Fourteenth Amendment includes the privacy interests contained in the Fourth Amendment.

Even though the Fourteenth Amendment did not specifically mention searches and seizures, Justice Felix Frankfurter, writing the opinion in *Wolf,* reasoned that the Fourteenth Amendment incorporated the rights of the Fourth Amendment. Therefore, states were required from that time forward to follow the restrictions of the Fourth Amendment when enforcing their own laws. But the Court also decided in Wolf that the illegally seized evidence was admissible in a state court. State criminal laws include possession of illegal narcotics, armed robbery, assault, and murder. State laws are enforced by prosecutors (also called district attorneys or state attorneys) in state courts.

Fourth Amendment Now Applying to State Cases

After the *Wolf* case, although the Fourth Amendment applied to state cases, the exclusionary rule did not. That meant that if a state, county, or city police officer seized evidence illegally, the evidence was still admissible against defendants in most state courts. Then, in 1961, in the landmark decision *Mapp* v. *Ohio*, the Supreme Court overruled *Wolf* and extended the exclusionary rule to state cases.[15] From that day forward, all evidence illegally seized by police, for either a federal or a state case, could no longer be used as evidence against a defendant.

In all of the Fourth Amendment cases discussed so far, convicted defendants asked the Supreme Court to review the conduct of law enforcement authorities and other government agents. The Supreme Court had ruled long ago that the Fourth Amendment did not apply to searches conducted by private citizens. But are law enforcement officers and other government agents the only persons subject to the limitations of the Fourth Amendment? What about public school officials? Are they government agents because they are employed by the state government? Does the Fourth Amendment apply to them? These questions had not been completely answered yet. In the meantime, the state and federal courts struggled with possible answers—and they did not always agree.

Who Is Subject to the Fourth Amendment?

On one extreme were courts in the states of Alaska, California, and Texas. They held that public school

In 1949, in the case of *Wolf* v. *Colorado*, Justice Felix Frankfurter wrote the decision on behalf of the Supreme Court. The Court ruled that in the area of law enforcement the Fourth Amendment's restrictions also applied to individual states.

officials are not subject to the constraints of the Fourth Amendment.[16] Those state courts held that public school officials are not government agents but private parties who act *in loco parentis*—a Latin term meaning "in the place of a parent."[17] The doctrine of *in loco parentis*, more than two hundred years old, was explained in 1769:

> [The father] may also delegate part of his parental authority, during his life, to the tutor or schoolmaster, of his child; who is then *in loco parentis* and has such a portion of the power of the parent committed to his charge, *viz.* that of restraint and correction, as may be necessary to answer the purposes for which he is employed.[18]

The Fourth Amendment in Schools

Courts that followed the doctrine of *in loco parentis* believed that parents entrust their children to the care of the schools. The schools, in turn, were responsible not only for educating the children but also for protecting them while they were in the school's custody. Using the doctrine of *in loco parentis*, the courts in Alaska, California, and Texas held that teachers, similar to parents, should be left free to discipline their students and maintain order in the schools. The *in loco parentis* doctrine basically assumes that a student has no legitimate expectation of privacy in his or her personal property, such as purses, gym bags, or clothing. Because parents have authority to search their child's property at will and are not subject to the restrictions of the Fourth Amendment, some courts held that school officials are not subject to the Fourth Amendment either.

On the other side of the argument, other courts recognized that students do have a legitimate expectation of privacy in their personal belongings. For example, students at the very least need to bring to school certain items like keys, money, and school supplies. They may also carry purses, wallets, or bags that contain personal items like photographs or diaries. Does that mean that students give up all rights to privacy just because they bring the items onto school property? Many courts said no.

If students have an expectation of privacy in their personal property, where did that leave school officials and the Fourth Amendment? According to many courts, it meant that schools are subject to the Fourth Amendment. Now came the more difficult question: What standard would apply to school officials who conducted searches of a student's personal property? Probable cause, or a lesser standard?

One court in Louisiana held that the Fourth Amendment applies to searches by public school officials. It also found that any search of student property conducted by a school official who does not have probable cause—the strictest justification—is unreasonable under the Fourth Amendment.[19]

The majority of the courts, though, reached a middle ground. New York, Delaware, Florida, Illinois, Michigan, New Mexico, Washington, Wisconsin, and several federal courts held that the Fourth Amendment does apply to searches conducted by public school authorities.[20] But they also held that because of the special needs of the school environment—to train, educate, and maintain discipline—school officials do not need probable cause to search. These courts recognized the increasingly serious problems of drug use and violent crimes in schools. Searches would be upheld if the school official had a reasonable suspicion that the search would uncover evidence of either a violation of school disciplinary rules or a violation of a state or federal law.

The First Amendment in Schools

The First Amendment guarantees all citizens the right to religious freedom. In 1943 the Supreme Court examined how this affected the West Virginia Board of Education's regulation that required all teachers and students in public schools to salute and pledge allegiance to the American flag.[21] In the 1943 case of

Board of Education v. *Barnette*, children belonging to the religious organization Jehovah's Witnesses, had been expelled from school for refusing to salute the flag. Their religion did not allow this ceremony. School officials threatened to send the children to juvenile delinquent reformatories. The state of West Virginia brought criminal charges against some of the parents for causing the delinquency. In the *Barnette* case, the parents brought suit to restrain enforcement of the regulations.

The majority of the Justices on the Supreme Court found that the First Amendment prohibited the state from forcing students to salute the flag. They believed that the First Amendment's right of freedom of religion was so important that a state could not limit it by state-enacted regulations.

Twenty-five years later, in 1968, five Iowa public-school children—John Tinker, fifteen years old, Mary Beth Tinker, thirteen years old, Chris Eckhardt, sixteen years old, and two other students—were suspended from school for wearing black armbands as a way of protesting the Vietnam War. In *Tinker* v. *Des Moines* School District, the Supreme Court was again asked to review a case in which students' exercise of their First Amendment rights collided with school rules.[22] This time the First Amendment right involved free speech.

In powerful language, Justice Abe Fortas, writing the opinion for the Supreme Court, made it clear that students do not shed their constitutional rights at the schoolhouse gate:

> School officials do not possess absolute authority over their students. Students in school as well as out of school are "persons" under our Constitution. They are possessed of fundamental rights which the State must respect, just as they themselves must respect their obligations to the State.[23]

Fortas also made it clear, however, that "conduct by the student, in class or out of it, which for any reason . . . materially disrupts classwork or involves substantial disorder or invasion of the rights of others is, of course, not immunized by the constitutional guarantee of freedom of speech."[24]

In the *Tinker* case no evidence existed to indicate that any classes were interrupted or that there were any threats or acts of violence on school property as a result of the students wearing black armbands. The Supreme Court concluded that "our Constitution does not permit officials of the State to deny their form of expression."[25]

Justice Hugo Black had agreed with the majority opinion in the *Barnette* case. He strenuously objected to the Court's opinion in *Tinker*, however. According to Justice Black, the Supreme Court had never held that students have constitutional rights to freedom of speech or expression in school. Public school students, Justice Black wrote, are not "sent to the schools at public expense to broadcast political or any other views to educate and inform the public."[26] Rather, public schools are operated "to give students an opportunity to learn, not to talk politics by actual speech, or by 'symbolic' speech."[27]

Justice Black warned that students would soon believe it was their right to control the schools rather than the right of the states. "I, for one," he wrote, "am not fully persuaded that school pupils are wise enough, even with this Court's expert help from Washington, to run the . . . public school systems in our 50 states."[28]

Students' Rights versus Schools' Rights

The Supreme Court continued to address the collision of student and school rights involving other constitutional amendments. In *Goss* v. *Lopez* (1975), Ohio public high school students were suspended from school for misconduct.[29] Because the school had not given the students the chance to defend their actions at a hearing before suspending them, they appealed their suspensions. They argued that the Due Process Clause of the Fourteenth Amendment required that they be notified in advance and allowed an opportunity for a hearing before they could be suspended. The Supreme Court agreed.

Under Ohio law the students had a legitimate claim of entitlement to a public education. Ohio had chosen to extend the right to an education to its residents, even though it was not obligated to do so. As such, the Supreme Court held that the Fourteenth Amendment required due process (notice and a hearing) before the state could deprive a student of the right to attend school.

If the First and Fourteenth Amendments applied to public schools, did that mean that all constitutional amendments applied?

In 1977 the Supreme Court heard the case of *Ingraham* v. *Wright*.[30] In the 1970s corporal (physical) punishment was permitted in public schools in every state except Massachusetts and New Jersey. James Ingraham and Roosevelt Andrews were both students at the Charles R. Drew Junior High School in Dade County, Florida. They asked the Supreme Court to find that paddling a public-school student constituted cruel and unusual punishment in violation of the Eighth Amendment to the Constitution. The Eighth Amendment provides that "Excessive bail shall not be required, nor excessive fines imposed, nor cruel and unusual punishments inflicted."[31]

James Ingraham was slow to respond to his teacher's instructions. For this, he was hit twenty times with a paddle while he was held over a table in the principal's office. The beating caused a blood clot, and he could not attend school for several days. Likewise, Roosevelt Andrews was paddled on several occasions. Once it caused him to lose the use of his arm for a week. The general rule in states that allowed corporal punishment was that a teacher could use reasonable force to control, train, or educate a child. If the force was excessive or unreasonable, the teacher could be held liable for money damages or be subject to criminal prosecution.

James Ingraham's and Roosevelt Andrews's attorneys acknowledged that the original purpose of the Eighth Amendment was to limit criminal punishments. They argued, though, that the amendment should also be extended to the paddling of schoolchildren. They pointed out that if the Eighth Amendment did not apply to schoolchildren, then schoolchildren could be beaten without any constitutional remedy, while hardened criminals in prison would have a remedy.

Supreme Court Justice Lewis Powell delivered the opinion for the Court. The Supreme Court found that the Eighth Amendment did not apply to the paddling of schoolchildren. Justice Powell wrote that "[t]he prisoner and the schoolchild stand in wholly different circumstances, separated by the harsh facts of criminal conviction and incarceration."[32] According to Justice Powell and the majority of the Court, "[t]he school-child has little need for the protection of the Eighth Amendment" because other legal remedies, such as money damages or criminal prosecution of teachers safeguards them from receiving excessive punishment.[33]

The Fourth Amendment and Public Schools

How would the Supreme Court view a request to apply the Fourth Amendment to public-school officials? Would the Fourth Amendment carry the same weight as the First and Fourteenth Amendments had in *Tinker* and *Barnette*? Or would the Court conclude that the rights afforded by the Fourth Amendment did not apply to schoolchildren, as it had about the Eighth Amendment in *Ingraham*? If the Fourth Amendment did apply, what justification for a search of student property would be necessary, probable cause or reasonable suspicion? Finally, if the search violated the Fourth Amendment, would the evidence seized be admissible at a criminal trial against the student defendant?

The state of New Jersey decided to seek answers from the Supreme Court. The New Jersey government asked the Supreme Court to review a case based on a

1980 incident at a high school in Piscataway. A math teacher named Ms. Chen walked into the girls' bathroom and saw two girls holding what she thought to be lit cigarettes. One of the girls was a fourteen-year-old freshman with the initials T.L.O. Smoking was permitted in certain designated areas in the school, but not in the lavatories. Chen escorted T.L.O. and the other girl to the principal's office and told the assistant vice principal, Theodore Choplick, what she had seen.

Choplick asked the girls whether they had been smoking in the lavatory. The girl who was with T.L.O. admitted she had been smoking. Choplick assigned her to a three-day smoking clinic.

T.L.O., on the other hand, answered not only that she had not been smoking in the lavatory but also that she did not smoke at all. Based on what Chen had told him, Choplick decided to investigate further. He directed T.L.O. to his private office. He closed the door and T.L.O. sat down in a chair in front of his desk. Choplick sat down at his desk and then asked T.L.O. to turn over her purse. She complied.

When Choplick opened T.L.O.'s purse he saw a package of Marlboro cigarettes sitting right on top. He picked up the package, held them up, and said to T.L.O., "You lied to me." As Choplick removed the cigarettes, he saw a package of rolling papers for cigarettes.

When he confronted T.L.O. with the rolling papers, she denied they belonged to her.

Choplick's experience as a school administrator had taught him that rolling papers were a sign that a person might smoke marijuana, so he continued looking through T.L.O.'s purse. He found a metal smoking pipe, one plastic bag of what he believed to be marijuana, and a wallet containing forty dollars in one-dollar bills. Inside a separate compartment of the purse he found two letters and an index card. The index card read "People who owe me money"; it was followed by a list of names and amounts of one dollar fifty cents and one dollar. Choplick read the letters, one from T.L.O. to another student and a return letter, and they indicated to him that T.L.O. was selling drugs.

Choplick called T.L.O.'s mother, then he called the police. T.L.O.'s mother agreed to take T.L.O. to the police station for questioning.

Once at the headquarters, a police officer advised T.L.O. of her rights. Under the landmark Supreme Court case *Miranda* v. *Arizona*, she had a right to remain silent and not answer any questions. She also had a right to an attorney, and anything she said to the police could be used against her at a trial.[34] T.L.O. signed a document stating that she would answer questions without an attorney.

In her mother's presence, T.L.O. admitted to the police that all of the items Choplick found inside her purse belonged to her. She also admitted that she had been selling marijuana in school for one dollar per joint, or marijuana cigarette. She had sold between eighteen and twenty joints at school that morning. Based on T.L.O.'s confession and the evidence Choplick had seized from her purse, the state of New Jersey filed a formal complaint against her in the Juvenile and Domestic Relations Court of Middlesex County. The complaint charged her with possession of marijuana with the intent to distribute. In juvenile cases, state law requires that the juvenile's name remain confidential, so the complaint used only T.L.O.'s initials, not her full name.

T.L.O.'s lawyer asked the juvenile court to apply the exclusionary rule and suppress the evidence Choplick had seized.[35] The lawyer argued that Choplick violated T.L.O.'s Fourth Amendment right to privacy when he searched her purse. The juvenile court denied T.L.O.'s motion to suppress the evidence and found her to be delinquent.

T.L.O. appealed the decision to a higher court but lost. She then appealed to the New Jersey Supreme Court. The court determined that a warrantless search of student property by a public-school official does not violate the Fourth Amendment. This is true as long as the school official has reasonable grounds to believe that a student possesses evidence of illegal activity or activity that would disrupt school discipline and order.

The court then found that Choplick had only a "good hunch" that T.L.O. was carrying cigarettes in her purse. No one, not even the math teacher, had said that they had actually seen cigarettes in her purse. According to the court, Choplick did not have a reasonable suspicion that he would find evidence of a school violation or a crime inside T.L.O.'s purse. Therefore, any evidence he seized from the purse should not have been admitted into evidence at her trial. The New Jersey Supreme Court reversed T.L.O.'s conviction.

The state of New Jersey did not give up. It appealed the case to the United States Supreme Court. The Supreme Court ruled, first, that the Fourth Amendment applied to searches and seizures conducted by public-school officials. The Justices also agreed that Choplick's search of the purse was reasonable and did not violate the Fourth Amendment.

The next step was for the Supreme Court to determine what legal standard justifies searches by a public-school official. Did the school official need a warrant? Did the school official need probable cause to search? Was some other lesser standard acceptable?

Chief Justice Warren Burger headed the Supreme Court that issued the
T.L.O. decision. In its decision, the Court ruled that in school searches,
public school officials, unlike law enforcement officers, need *not* have
probable cause.

The Justices agreed that warrants were not suited to the school environment and would interfere with swift discipline. They then concluded that the search needed only to be reasonable. Unlike law enforcement officers, public school officials did not need probable cause. Finally, they found that Choplick acted reasonably when he searched T.L.O.'s purse. A teacher had reported seeing T.L.O. smoking in the girls' bathroom; this gave Choplick reason to believe T.L.O. might have cigarettes in her purse. Choplick's discovery of rolling papers then gave him a reasonable suspicion that T.L.O. was carrying marijuana in her purse. That suspicion justified a further look. When that search turned up a pipe, a number of plastic bags, a small quantity of marijuana, and a fairly substantial amount of money, it was not unreasonable for Choplick to extend his search to the zippered compartment.

The United States Supreme Court reversed the New Jersey Supreme Court's judgment. T.L.O.'s conviction for delinquency would stand.

Was Suspicion of Wrongdoing Always Required?

In *T.L.O.*, the vice principal suspected T.L.O. of wrongdoing. Later cases decided by the United States Supreme Court made it clear, though, that suspicion of

Justices uphold searches and limit student rights

By ROBERT COHEN
Star-Ledger Washington Bureau

WASHINGTON—The Supreme Court ruled yesterday that teachers and principals may search students if they reasonably believe that there has been a violation of the law or school rules.

In a 6-3 decision involving a former New Jersey schoolgirl, the court concluded that students in school are protected by the constitutional guarantee against unreasonable searches, but not to the same degree as adults facing searches by police.

The court said a student's legitimate expectation of privacy in school is not ironclad and must be balanced against the need of school officials to maintain order and discipline.

Justice Byron White, writing for the majority, said searches of students in school will be justified "when there are reasonable grounds for suspecting

that the search will turn up evidence that the student has violated or is violating either the law or the rules of the school."

White said the search must be "reasonable under the circumstances" and "not excessively intrusive in light of the age and sex of the student and the nature of the infraction."

The justice said a stricter standard used by police in searches of adults would be too burdensome in the school setting. In adult cases, police must have "probable cause" that an individual has violated or is violating the law in order to conduct a search.

Although maintaining their standard is similar to the one adopted in 1983 by the New Jersey Supreme Court, the justices reversed the state tribunal and concluded that a vice principal at Piscataway High School acted reasonably in 1980 when he searched the pocketbook of a 14-year-old identified only as T.L.O.

T.L.O was reported by a teacher to have been smoking in the restroom in violation of school rules. After she denied the charge, Assistant Vice Principal Theodore Choplick opened her purse and found cigarettes as well as marijuana paraphernalia and evidence she might be selling marijuana.

The teenager was subsequently prosecuted for delinquency, but the charges were thrown out after the New Jersey Supreme Court said the search was unreasonable and illegal.

White, whose decision reinstates the finding of delinquency, said Choplick's decision to search the purse to look for cigarettes was a "common sense conclusion." Once he saw the marijuana paraphernalia, White said, "this suspicion justified further exploration of T.L.O.'s purse."

White was joined by Chief Justice Warren

Please turn to Page 10

The *T.L.O.* decision upheld student searches and limited students' rights.

wrongdoing was not always required to justify a search. In 1989 the Supreme Court upheld suspicionless searches to conduct drug testing of railroad employees who had been involved in train accidents in *Skinner* v. *Railroad Labor Executives' Association*.[36] Also in 1989, it upheld random drug testing of federal customs officers who carry guns in the case of *Treasury Employees* v. *Von Raab*.[37] In 1990 it upheld automobile checkpoints set up by police officers to look for drunk drivers in *Michigan Department of State Police* v. *Sitz*.[38]

Now it was clear that the Fourth Amendment applied to school searches and that officials needed only reasonable suspicion to justify such searches. How would the Acton family's case be affected by the Supreme Court's decision to allow suspicionless searches? Would the Supreme Court extend those cases to the school setting? Would the Supreme Court allow random drug testing when school officials had no reason to believe that a particular student was using illegal drugs? The Vernonia School District and the Actons decided to find out.

3

The Case for the
Vernonia School District

ACLU attorney Thomas M. Christ filed a lawsuit against the Vernonia School District. To begin a lawsuit, the plaintiff, or complainant, must file a formal complaint with a court. In this case, the complaint named Wayne and Judy Acton, the guardians of James Acton, as plaintiffs. The Vernonia School District was named as the defendant.

Types of Lawsuits

There are many different types of lawsuits, called actions. Some are criminal actions, filed by a state or federal attorney, called a prosecutor, on behalf of the people. In less serious criminal cases, called misdemeanors, the prosecutor may file a document known as an information. This document charges a defendant with a particular crime, such as shoplifting or simple assault.

In more serious criminal actions, called felonies, the prosecutor must first obtain an indictment. To obtain an indictment, the prosecutor must present evidence about the case to a grand jury. What is a grand jury and what does it mean to be indicted?

A grand jury is a group of citizens who are summoned together by the government to hear the testimony of witnesses and examine evidence. The grand jury's job is to determine whether a suspect should be charged with a particular crime. The grand jurors must decide two things based on the evidence presented to them: (1) whether there is probable cause to believe that a crime has been committed, and (2) whether it is likely that the suspect is the person who committed the crime. If it decides that the suspect should be prosecuted, the grand jury will formally charge the suspect in a document called an indictment.

A grand jury should not be confused with a petit jury. Unlike petit jurors, grand jurors do not decide if a suspect is guilty or not guilty; they only decide whether there is enough evidence to proceed with the case. Petit jurors, on the other hand, actually attend the trial, hear the evidence, and render a verdict in the case. Unlike the proceedings in a trial courtroom, the only persons allowed in the grand jury room are the grand jurors, the prosecutor, and the witness who is testifying. There is no judge, defense attorney, or defendant. Also, all grand jury deliberations are secret, whereas trial court proceedings, with very few exceptions, are open to the public.

Other lawsuits are called civil actions. Examples of civil actions include claims of breach of contract, personal injuries, and damage to property. There are also civil actions called declaratory actions. In this type of lawsuit a plaintiff asks the court to make a legal ruling in the plaintiff's favor. Sometimes a plaintiff will also ask for injunctive relief as part of a declaratory action. This means that the plaintiff asks the court to stop the defendant from doing something in particular.

The Actons' Lawsuit

On November 4, 1991, Thomas Christ filed the Actons' lawsuit in the United States District Court for the District of Oregon, a federal trial court. The complaint asked for declaratory and injunctive relief. Specifically, the complaint asked the court to rule that the school district's drug testing policy was unlawful because it violated James's rights under the Fourth and

Fourteenth Amendments to the United States Constitution. The complaint also asked the court to enjoin, stop, the school district from enforcing the policy and from interfering with James's participation in school athletic programs.

The Vernonia School District hired the law firm of Lane, Powell, Spears & Lubersky to answer the complaint. Every defendant must file a written answer to a complaint; if the complaint is not answered, the court will assume that the defendant does not contest the suit. The court will then enter a judgment in favor of the plaintiff. This type of judgment is called a default judgment.

The Vernonia School District, through its lawyers, responded to the complaint. It admitted that it had adopted the student athlete drug policy mentioned in the plaintiffs' complaint. It also admitted that it had refused to allow James Acton to participate in school-sponsored athletic programs because he did not comply with the policy.

The next part of the school district's answer listed its "affirmative defenses." This is the part of an answer that does more than just respond to the plaintiff's complaints; it asserts a defendant's specific defenses. In the *Vernonia* case, the school district stated in its defense that the drug testing policy was rationally related to the school district's interest in the health, safety, well-being, and education of its students. It also asserted that the school district's actions were in good faith and lawful.

The Trial

The case was assigned to federal judge Malcolm F. Marsh. Judge Marsh would hear the testimony and judge the case without the presence of a jury. The Vernonia School District wanted to convince Judge Marsh that it had valid reasons for enforcing its drug policy. Attorneys A. Gregg Powell and Chris L. Mullman handled the trial on behalf of the school district. They called several school officials to testify about how the policy came into being and why it was important to the school district.

Powell first called Randy Aultman to testify. Aultman was the principal of Washington Grade School, where James Acton was enrolled. Aultman had formerly been the assistant superintendent of Vernonia School District. Before that, he had been the principal of Vernonia High School. Aultman was raised in Vernonia and described it to the judge as being a very solid logging community.

Aultman testified that sports played a "very, very big part" in the lives of Vernonia children.[1] About 60 percent of the high school students and 75 percent of the elementary students were involved in some type of sport. The community and parents of students frequently did volunteer work to finance athletic programs.

Aultman told of minor disciplinary problems in the high school in the early 1980s. About forty to fifty students were referred to the principal for discipline each year. During the 1988 and 1989 school years, however, he noticed an upswing in drug use by high school students. Aultman said that "[k]ids were blatantly oftentimes talking about that they used drugs and there was nothing school officials could do."[2] Aultman was shocked to learn from a football coach that a large number of athletes were openly admitting to drug use. During the 1988–89 school year, between 100 and 110 students were referred to the principal for disciplinary problems. Students told him that they were using marijuana, alcohol, and amphetamines.

Parents, the community, and the school board became very concerned. According to Aultman, they were facing "some epidemic proportions of drug usage."[3] The school began efforts to educate students about drugs. It hired guest speakers who told the students about their problems with drugs. The school also brought in drug-sniffing dogs to check student lockers.

Nothing seemed to work, though. Students were still using drugs, and many of them were suspended.

Aultman testified that the school district wanted a drug policy because it was concerned about the safety of the students; it was not interested in expelling kids from school. Because it wanted a prevention program, the school district developed the drug testing program for school athletes.

Thomas Christ, who represented the Actons, had the opportunity to question Aultman, too. When an attorney for the opposing party questions that party's witness, it is called cross-examination. Aultman admitted during cross-examination that he had no reason to suspect that James Acton was using drugs. Aultman also admitted that the school's current search and seizure policy allowed the school to search student property *only* if the school had reasonable suspicion of wrong-doing by the student.

After Aultman testified, the school district's attorney called several other witnesses who were teachers in Vernonia. Teacher and athletic director Marcia King testified that she noticed an increase in injuries to athletes in the late 1980s. Wrestling coach Ronald Svenson described a serious injury to an athlete that he suspected was the result of the student smoking marijuana. He was particularly concerned because he had heard of the deaths of Len Bias and Don Rogers. (Len Bias was a college basketball player from the University of Maryland who was drafted by the NBA's Boston Celtics and later died of a cocaine overdose. Don Rogers was a professional football player with the Cleveland Browns who had also died of a drug overdose.)

King and Svenson saw students passing marijuana cigarettes back and forth to each other in a small café across the street from the high school. They also overheard students talking about drug use and noticed that they were louder and more hostile in class. After the school district adopted the drug testing policy, though, King noticed a considerable decrease in disciplinary problems.

Kathleen Sevig was also a teacher at Vernonia High School. She testified that in the late 1980s, she noticed tremendous behavioral changes in her students. She characterized them as "students who were much more hostile, who wanted to dominate the classroom, whose behavior was very erratic and . . . very, very gross and inappropriate."[4] King told of students using profane language, being loud in the hallways, shouting, and banging their heads into the lockers as hard as they could.

Sevig, like the other teachers, noticed a major change after the school adopted the drug testing program. The disciplinary problems decreased to only a few, and she no longer sensed any hostility by the students in her classroom.

In addition to the testimony of actual witnesses, the trial court had copies of the deposition of expert witness Dr. Robert L. DuPont. In a civil action, during a period called discovery, parties are allowed to examine and investigate what evidence the opposing party intends to present at trial. One of the ways to discover the information is to record the sworn testimony of a witness. Sworn testimony occurs when a witness takes an oath to tell the truth before giving his or her testimony. This form of discovery is called a deposition.

DuPont testified that a drug test is the only reliable way to determine whether a person is impaired by drugs. He also said that drug use increases the risk of accidents since people who use drugs often become careless. The effect can be unpredictable, though. In other words, a person may use drugs ten times or one hundred times before that person has a health problem or causes an injury.

It is a general rule of law that witnesses are not permitted to give their opinions about a particular subject. They can only testify about what they personally have seen or experienced. Expert witnesses are the exceptions to this rule, however. Expert witnesses are those people the court determines to have a higher level of education and expertise in a particular subject.

Dr. DuPont was called as an expert witness for the Vernonia School District. That meant that he was allowed to give his opinion about the subject of risk of injury to a student who uses drugs. DuPont gave his opinion that a student who tests positive for the presence of cocaine, marijuana, or amphetamines is under a substantial risk of injury to himself or to others.

Judge Marsh's Decision

On May 7, 1992, Judge Marsh issued his decision in the case of *Acton* v. *Vernonia School District.*[5] (The Acton's, as the party that initially brought the suit to court, had their name listed first.) In a nonjury trial the judge is the only person who has had the opportunity to see and hear the witnesses, so it is important for the judge to state in the decision whether the witnesses were found to be credible. If the case is appealed to a higher court, that appellate court will rely on the trial court's findings on the credibility of each witness.

Judge Marsh found the witnesses to be truthful. He was also impressed by the teachers' knowledge and concern for the community, its students, and the school system.

Judge Marsh wrote a lengthy opinion. In it, he cited

many of the cases that had reached the United States Supreme Court in the years preceding *Acton*. He also described the case of *Schaill* v. *Tippecanoe County School District* that was heard by a federal court of appeals in 1989.[6] In *Schaill* several students had challenged the constitutionality of the school system's random drug testing program for athletes. The federal court of appeals in that case found that the program was reasonable because of the following findings:

- The testing was random.
- The program was not intended to punish athletes.
- Drug use posed a particular threat to athletes.
- There was evidence of student injuries caused by drug use.
- Other methods did not solve the problem.
- Student athletes were routinely subjected to events of a public nature.
- The testing and the test results were private.

Judge Marsh noted another random drug testing case, *Derdeyn* v. *University of Colorado*, which had a different result. In *Derdeyn*, decided by the Colorado Court of Appeals in 1991, the court held that the university's interest in a drug-free athletic program was not compelling.[7] In addition, the drug testing procedures violated the athletes' Fourth Amendment rights. The

Derdeyn decision was similar to cases that had been decided in California, Arkansas, and Texas.[8] In those cases, however, the facts were not the same as they were in *Vernonia.* The California court found that the drug testing program violated students' privacy. The Arkansas court found that the test results were unreliable. In Texas, the school district wanted to drug test students who participated in any extracurricular activity. The Texas court found there was no connection between drug use and injuries sustained during extracurricular activities.

Judge Marsh ruled that Vernonia School District's drug testing policy was reasonable. First, he cited the testimony of coaches who had observed athletes performing poorly and unsafely while under the influence of drugs. Then, he noted evidence that athletes were role models and leaders for the entire community. If the leaders were deterred from using drugs, Judge Marsh wrote, then it was reasonable to believe that other students would also be deterred.

The judge also concluded that because the drug policy was limited to athletes, it was not a "fishing expedition" for school administrators. Also, the school district had tried other methods, but they did not work. Finally, the testing was done privately, and the test results remained confidential. Judge Marsh concluded that the drug testing policy did not violate a student's rights under the Fourth Amendment.

He also considered the issue under the Oregon Constitution, which states:

> No law shall violate the right of the people to be secure in their persons, house, papers, and effects, against unreasonable search, or seizure; and no warrant shall issue but upon probable cause, supported by oath, or affirmation, and particularly describing the place to be searched, and the person or thing to be seized.

There were no Oregon state cases directly addressing the type of search the Vernonia School District wanted to conduct. However, Judge Marsh cited other Oregon cases that upheld warrantless checkpoint stops to check hunting licenses and warrantless searches of certain businesses to check for safety violations. The judge cited the same reasons for his conclusion that the drug testing policy in *Vernonia* did not violate a student's rights under the Fourth Amendment. He concluded again that the Vernonia School District's drug testing policy was reasonable under the Oregon Constitution.

The Vernonia School District had won the first round in court. Judge Marsh upheld the district's drug testing policy. He denied the Actons' request to stop the school from conducting drug tests.

The Appeal

The Actons continued to pursue their claim. They decided to appeal their case to a higher court. When a party loses in the federal district court, it is entitled to appeal the case to the United States Court of Appeals. The United States Court of Appeals is divided into regional circuits, or sections. Each circuit has jurisdiction, meaning authority, over certain federal district courts. The Ninth Circuit has jurisdiction over all federal trial courts in the states of Oregon, Washington, Idaho, Montana, Nevada, Alaska, Arizona, Hawaii, and California. Therefore, the Actons had to make their appeal to the United States Court of Appeals for the Ninth Circuit.

Appealing their case meant that the Actons had to file a brief, a written statement of arguments, explaining their legal theories. Vernonia had to respond to the brief. Attorneys Powell and Mullman wrote the brief on behalf of Vernonia and filed it with the appellate court. But, in an unusual turn of events, Powell and Mullman did not present oral arguments to the court. Both Powell and Mullman left the law firm where they were employed before the oral argument was scheduled by the court. Another attorney, Timothy R. Volpert, argued Vernonia's case to the panel of judges.

For most appeals in federal cases, three judges hear

Timothy R. Volpert argued the case for the Vernonia School District on appeal to the judges of the Ninth Circuit Court.

the case and render a decision. Ninth Circuit judges Stephen Reinhardt, Melvin Brunetti, and Ferdinand F. Fernandez were assigned to handle the case for the Vernonia School District.

After hearing oral arguments and reading the briefs, the Ninth Circuit issued an opinion. The appellate court first grappled with the Oregon Constitution. Under federal law, if a provision of a state constitution is basically the same as a provision of the United States Constitution, the federal appellate court can decide the case using the United States Constitution. If the state constitution gives more protection to a citizen, then the federal appellate court must decide the case based on the state constitution.

Whether to use the Oregon Constitution or the United States Constitution was not entirely clear to the United States Court of Appeals for the Ninth Circuit. It concluded that it might refer to some Oregon law but should decide this case based on federal law and the Fourth Amendment to the United States Constitution.

The appellate court determined first, as the two courts before it, that drug testing is a search under the Fourth Amendment. Second, the appellate court noted that neither the Actons nor Vernonia had challenged whether the warrantless search was authorized.

Warrantless searches are generally illegal. However, some exceptions to that rule are as follows:

- If the person consents to the search.
- If the evidence is in plain view.
- If an officer has reason to stop and frisk a suspect.
- If a lawmaking body authorizes the search.

The Ninth Circuit found that the search was properly authorized by a lawmaking body.

Next the court considered whether the drug testing program was reasonable. It disagreed with the trial court's finding that student athletes do not have as much of an expectation of privacy as other students. It also wrote that children may be compelled to attend school, but they do not totally lose their right to privacy. It finally concluded that Vernonia's policy might justify individualized testing but it did not justify random testing. It did not agree with the Seventh Circuit court of appeals in the *Tippecanoe County* case that an almost identical drug testing program was reasonable. The United States Court of Appeals reversed the trial court's decision.[9]

Vernonia School District was back where it started. It requested that the appellate court reconsider the case, but the court refused to do so.

The Appeal to the United States Supreme Court

The Vernonia School District had only one alternative: It could appeal the decision to the court of last resort— the United States Supreme Court. Attorney Volpert continued to handle the case.

The first step Volpert had to take to have Vernonia's case heard by the United States Supreme Court was to file a legal document called a petition for writ of *certiorari*, a Latin term that means "to be made certain."[10] A petition for writ of *certiorari* calls "for delivery to a higher court of the record of a proceeding before a lower court."[11] The document generally describes the legal issues that the party, now called the petitioner, wants the higher court to review. The respondents, in this case the Actons, are allowed to file an opposing brief urging the Supreme Court not to grant the petition. If the Supreme Court decides that the legal issues in the case require its review, then it will agree to hear the case and will grant the petition. The Supreme Court—the highest court in the country—generally selects to hear only those cases that present new federal legal issues, or ones in which there is a conflict among appellate courts around the country as to how the legal issue should be resolved.

Volpert's petition gave three reasons for requesting

that the Supreme Court hear Vernonia's case. First, it argued that the Ninth Circuit's holding conflicted with a Seventh Circuit holding in *Schaill* v. *Tippecanoe County School District.* In that case the federal court of appeals had held that a similar drug testing program was reasonable under the Fourth Amendment. Volpert also pointed out the Supreme Court's ruling in *New Jersey* v. *T.L.O.*, upon which the Court in the *Schaill* v. *Tippecanoe County School District* relied. In *T.L.O.* the Supreme Court upheld a warrantless search of a student's purse.

Next, Volpert pointed out that the *Vernonia* case was a good opportunity for the Supreme Court to expand its ruling in *New Jersey* v. *T.L.O.* One of the issues of concern in the *Vernonia* case was that the drug testing program affected all student athletes, regardless of whether they were individually suspected of using drugs. The Supreme Court had noted in *T.L.O.*, however, that the Fourth Amendment imposes no requirement of individualized suspicion. Suspicion by a school official that a particular student had committed a crime or violated a school regulation was not necessary. Volpert asked the Supreme Court to find that the Vernonia School District did not have to suspect an individual athlete of drug use before it could require a drug test.

Volpert then argued that educating children in an environment free of drugs, excessive discipline problems, and a heightened risk of physical injury justifies drug testing of student athletes. He again cited the *T.L.O.* case, in which Justice Powell said that a state has a "compelling interest" in educating and training its young people.[12]

The Acton family, through ACLU attorney Christ, opposed Volpert's petition for writ of *certiorari*. The United States Supreme Court granted the writ on November 28, 1994. That meant that Volpert would have to prepare a full brief and the ACLU would have an opportunity to respond.

Volpert addressed the same issue he had up to this point—whether drug testing of student athletes can be reasonable under the Fourth Amendment in the absence of individualized suspicion. He reminded the Supreme Court that it had upheld searches that were not based on individualized suspicion in several other cases. In those cases the Supreme Court had balanced the governmental interest in the search, the individual's expectation of privacy, and the effectiveness of the search.

Volpert then argued that the Vernonia School District had a compelling interest in protecting the safety of its student athletes. It also had an interest in protecting the educational environment of its schools. He pointed out that Vernonia had tried other methods to correct the drug problem, but none had worked. The drug testing policy, Volpert claimed, was not a great intrusion on a student's privacy because the testing itself was done privately in the bathroom and because the test results remained confidential. Finally, he argued that students did not *have* to be subjected to the drug test. If a student did not want to be drug tested, he or she could opt not to play sports.

In some cases before the United States Supreme Court, a person or group other than the original parties will volunteer or will be invited by the Supreme Court to file a separate brief giving advice on the pending matter. These groups are known as *amici curiae*, friends of the court.[13] In the *Vernonia* case, many other groups that supported the Vernonia School District offered their advice to the Court. Some of the groups included the National School Boards Association, the American Alliance for Rights and Responsibilities, and the Criminal Justice Legal Foundation. The United States Department of Justice also submitted a brief in support of the Vernonia School District. Richard H. Seamon, one of the government attorneys who helped write the justice department's brief, would later find himself arguing the case to the Supreme Court.

Jerseyans split on the ruling

Kathy Rossi
'Not sure how I feel'

Saul Cooperman
'I applaud decision'

By JUDY PEET

Reflecting the disagreement among the justices of the nation's highest court, educators, students and parents across the state were also at odds in their reactions to the ruling expanding a school administrator's power to search students.

Comments ranged from "fantastic" to "a constitutional travesty" on the U.S. Supreme Court's 6-3 ruling that schoolchildren do not have the same rights to privacy as adults and can be freely searched if there is reasonable suspicion the student has violated either the law or school regulations.

"Although there is always concern about possible abuses, I applaud the Supreme Court decision and I think the overwhelming majority of school officials will handle the situation with sensitivity," state Commissioner of Education Saul Cooperman commented.

Jennifer Powell
'They have a right'

Please turn to Page 16

Reaction is split among Jersey educators, pupils and school officials

Continued from Page 1

"The protection of the school community has got to be the first consideration of any administrator, even if it means giving up some rights of the minority," Cooperman added.

"Of course, this should not be interpreted as carte blanche to publicly humiliate a student, but I don't think that will happen.

"I think students will see little change in school policies, and I certainly don't think this will open the door to any kind of shakedowns," he stated.

Also in favor of the decision was James Koch, principal of Piscataway High School, where a 1980 pocketbook search of a 14-year-old identified as T.L.O. launched the court battle leading to yesterday's ruling.

Calling the decision "fantastic," Koch added: "It really says that educators who care, who are really trying to check on all the things that students might bring in that could be harmful, are doing a good job."

The defendant, now 19, who has since graduated high school and works as a secretary, could not be reached for comment. However, her attorney, Public Defender Lois DeJulio, maintained the federal ruling "doesn't open the door for abuses of student rights, it closes them.

"Before, no one would even admit a schoolchild had rights," DeJulio explained. "At least now, we have accepted children do have Fourth Amendment protections and at least the Supreme Court didn't totally kiss their privacy good-by."

DeJulio, who characterized her young client as "very shy and not at all comfortable with being a test case," said she will consider taking the case back to the state Supreme Court "because the (federal) ruling did not address the definition of 'reasonable' sus-

Eric Hegg
'It's ridiculous'

picion as it applies under state law."

The attorney added T.L.O. will not be affected by the reversal of the state court decision, because the teenager has fulfilled the probationary terms of her 1982 conviction.

Ironically, while DeJulio lauded the federal justices for expanding student rights, her opponent, state Deputy Attorney General Alan Nodes also hailed the panel for restricting those protections.

"We are very happy with the ruling. In essence, it says if teachers want to search a student, they can," Nodes said.

"You can't just walk up to a student and stick your hand in their pocket," he explained. "But you can stick your hand in his pocket if you inspect there is contraband, like cigarettes, there."

Anthony Procopio, assistant principal of Marlboro High School, and Joseph Kruczek, assistant principal of

Hendrik Arden
'Abide by rules'

Manalapan High School, both recently addressed the question of student rights as representatives of the Freehold Regional High School District, the largest secondary district in the state.

"We've been watching for this decision," Procopio said. "It is absolutely imperative that school districts have the right to inspect students lockers, if necessary, for the safety of the entire school."

Kruczek agreed, noting: "It's about time when they placed the welfare and education of the youth in the hands of the school administrators that they give us the legal right to protect the students."

Of several school administrators contacted yesterday, the group unilaterally echoed Cooperman's endorsement of the high court ruling, but that was not the case across the board.

"I agree that going to school is a privilege, not a right, but denying a student of his or her rights is a travesty of

Vicki Newman
'How is parent to react?'

the Constitution, nothing less," maintained Sal Guadagnino, who has taught science for 19 years at New Providence High School.

"Given the mentality of far too many school administrators, and the vagueness of the ruling, this situation can and will be abused," Guadagnino stated.

"I can see it opening the door for outright harassment of any student unfortunate enough to be labeled 'troublemaker.'"

"It's ridiculous," said Eric Hegg, a student at Morristown High School.

"They should have no more right to search you in school than they do to come into your home. It's not right."

Several students said that school officials should have "solid proof" of

Richard Fiander
'Act accordingly'

wrongdoing before being allowed to conduct searches.

Morristown High School sophomores William McKay and Hendrik Arden agreed that proof of wrongdoing should be necessary prior to a search by school officials. But Arden also argued that students complying with school regulations would have no cause for concern.

"If you go to school, you should abide by the rules," said Arden. "If you don't abide by the rules, then I guess you should fear a search."

Other students polled yesterday, at the Menlo Park Mall in Edison, had a much more conservative reaction.

"I think they do have a right to search students, and it wouldn't do any good if they told you beforehand," said 13-year-old Jennifer Powell, an 8th-grader at Rahway Junior High School.

"I guess it's okay," said shy 13-year-old Laura Rossi of Middlesex, who looked to her mother, Kathy, for guid-

ance on the question.

"I'm really not sure how I feel about it," Rossi admitted.

"On one hand, if a student is old enough to know what's going on, I think they should know better than to put anything in their locker, and I am for them being searched.

"On the other hand, once they decide to pick on a kid, he's had it," she added. "It also seems that the rights of the parents in protecting their kids aren't really being considered."

Vicki Newman, whose son is a sophomore at Scotch Plains-Fanwood High School, said she was "confused. How is a parent supposed to react?

"I think searches are right and if a kid gets caught, he knew he was taking a 'risk,'" she explained. "But how does protecting anybody have anything to do with silly stuff, like whether a kid has cigarettes in his pocket. Maybe they've gone too far."

How far teachers and administrators will be allowed to go in determining "reasonable" suspicion for a search is a major question left unanswered by the U.S. Supreme Court.

In the absence of such interpretation, Richard Fiander, superintendent of the Summit school district, said he will stick with the guidelines his district put into effect this year.

"I think our rules fit very comfortably with what I understand of the definition of reasonable suspicion," Fiander said.

"We have six factors: The source of information on any sort of wrongdoing; the age of the youngster; his school history; recent behavior; the seriousness of the suspected wrongdoing, and what we call exigency—that is, how important is it to act this minute, or is there time to contact parents first.

"You don't go through this over a pack of cigarettes," Fiander stated. "But if the problem is serious, you weigh the factors and act accordingly."

In his arguments for the Vernonia School District, attorney Timothy R. Volpert cited the circumstances in the *T.L.O.* decision.

After filing their briefs, the Vernonia School District and the other supportive organizations (friends of the court) waited for the Actons' response. How would the ACLU address the issue raised? What would the Actons' attorneys say to make their case? Would James Acton be required to submit to a drug test?

4

The Case for the Actons

When the school would not permit James Acton to play football because he and his parents refused to sign the consent form for drug testing, Wayne and Judy Acton sought help from the American Civil Liberties Union (ACLU). The Actons did not have money to pay an attorney, but that did not matter; the ACLU keeps a list of private attorneys who handle cases *pro bono*, or without pay. Attorney Thomas M. Christ's name was on that list.

Christ had been practicing law in a private law firm in Portland, Oregon, for about eight years. He had always been interested in civil rights issues and decided to volunteer his services to the ACLU. When the executive director of the local office of the ACLU asked him to take the Actons' case, he accepted.

Wayne and Judy Acton told Christ that they were concerned about the message the Vernonia School District was sending to their son, James. Since James did not use drugs, the Actons believed that it was wrong for the school to force him to take a drug test when there was no suspicion of drug use. Wayne and Judy discussed the matter with James, and they decided as a family to fight the drug testing policy.

Christ filed a formal complaint against the Vernonia School District in the United States District Court for the District of Oregon. Vernonia's attorney responded to the complaint, and the case was set for trial.

James was called to testify in federal court about his case, and he swore to tell the truth. When Christ asked him why he did not want to take the drug test, James said, "Because I feel that they have no reason to think I was taking drugs."[1]

Randy Aultman, the principal of Washington Grade School, and several other teachers and coaches described to the federal judge how the Vernonia School District had been experiencing a large increase in drug problems during the late 1980s. They told of how the schools had tried to curb the problems with guest speakers and other measures, none of which worked. Likewise, teachers complained of increasingly hostile, loud, and disobedient behavior by students.

Those complaints, the teachers and coaches testified, led to the school district's policy requiring drug testing of student athletes. After the policy was instituted, the teachers noticed a major change in the behavior of their students. There were far fewer disciplinary problems, and classes were back to normal for the most part.

Testimony given on cross-examination is as important as testimony on direct examination. Christ's cross-examination of Aultman and the teachers highlighted several key points.

Aultman made three interesting points when he was cross-examined by Christ. First, he testified that the Vernonia schools had a general search-and-seizure policy that permitted the school to search a student or the student's property if a school official had reasonable suspicion that the student had committed a crime or violated a school regulation. Aultman then admitted that no school official at the Washington Grade School had any reason to suspect James Acton of taking drugs. Aultman also admitted that he had not personally seen any student taking drugs.

Athletic director Marcia King also admitted during cross-examination that she had never seen a student take drugs and then immediately play sports.

Judge Malcolm F. Marsh was not persuaded by the information brought out during cross-examination. He ruled that the Vernonia School District drug testing policy did not violate a student's Fourth or Fourteenth Amendment rights. What would the Actons do now?

The Actons Appeal Their Case

The Actons had the right to appeal their case to the next highest court. In the federal system, that court is the United States Court of Appeals. Because the case was initially filed in a federal court in Oregon, jurisdiction over the appeal was in the United States Court of Appeals for the Ninth Circuit. On appeal, a case is decided based on written briefs filed by each party arguing his or her legal position and, in some cases, an oral argument presented by the attorneys to a panel of three appellate judges.

An appellate court must follow certain guidelines when reviewing the decision of a trial court. It reviews the trial court's rulings on the facts of the case and on the law. For example, when a trial court rules on the facts of the case, meaning that it finds that certain facts are true, an appellate court cannot reverse the trial court's ruling unless the ruling was clearly wrong. How does an appellate court determine whether a trial court's ruling was incorrect? The appellate court reviews all of the evidence presented at trial and will reverse the trial court only if it firmly believes that the trial court committed a mistake.

When an appellate court reviews a trial court's conclusions about the law, the appellate court reviews the case *de novo*, or anew. The appellate court determines the law of the case on its own and does not have to rely on the trial court's interpretation.

Christ filed his appellate brief on behalf of the Actons. In the meantime, because the district court had ruled against him, James Acton decided to take the drug test so he could play basketball. He then waited for the next round in court.

The Ninth Circuit heard the case on November 3, 1993. Circuit court judges Stephen Reinhardt, Melvin Brunetti, and Ferdinand F. Fernandez were assigned to hear and decide the case. The Actons' brief argued that the Vernonia School District had failed to prove that there was actually a drug problem. The Actons also argued that, even if there were a drug problem, it did not justify random testing of student athletes.

The United States Court of Appeals for the Ninth Circuit disagreed with the Actons' first argument. The trial court had found that the Vernonia School District presented sufficient evidence to establish that its schools had a drug problem. That ruling by the trial court was a "factual finding," which could only be reversed by the appellate court if it found that the judge clearly made a mistake.

The Actons argued that the trial judge relied on hearsay evidence that should not have been allowed at the trial. But the appellate court read the trial transcripts and noted that school administrators and faculty had presented ample evidence of drug usage by students. Therefore, the appellate court found that the trial court did not clearly make a mistake. The Ninth Circuit emphasized, however, that "what the evidence shows, and all it shows, is that there was some drug usage in the schools, that student discipline had declined, that athletes were involved, and that there was reason to believe that one athlete had suffered an injury because of drug usage and others may have."[2]

The appellate court then found that Vernonia's drug testing policy helped the school district reach its desired goal of improving discipline and decreasing drug use. The court was not so sure, however, that random drug testing of athletes was necessary to accomplish that goal.

The court did not agree with Vernonia's argument that athletes have a lower expectation of privacy than do other students. In addition, the court was not persuaded by Vernonia's argument that because participation in athletics is voluntary, privacy of athletes is reduced.

The court recognized that Vernonia's desires to prevent unnecessary athletic injuries, to reduce drug use among students, and to improve discipline were admirable. But the court did not agree that those goals were important enough to justify random drug testing of athletes. The court compared Vernonia's goals to those of federal agencies that had adopted drug testing policies to prevent airplane or train accidents or a gas pipeline or nuclear power plant disaster. However, the need for the school district's policy just did not seem to measure up to the dangers other drug testing policies sought to prevent.

After considering the governmental and privacy interests involved, the United States Court of Appeals for the Ninth Circuit reversed the trial court's ruling. It concluded that the Vernonia School District's random drug testing of athletes was unconstitutional. The school district suspended its drug testing program.

Vernonia Appeals the Ninth Circuit's Ruling

The Vernonia School District had suffered a setback. It decided to take its case all the way to the United States Supreme Court. It filed a petition for writ of *certiorari* asking the Supreme Court to hear the case. The Actons, through their lawyer, Thomas M. Christ, opposed the petition.

Christ listed eight reasons that the Supreme Court should decline to hear the case. For example, Christ wrote that the appellate court had decided the case based on the Oregon constitution, not the United States Constitution. The Supreme Court generally does not hear cases that are based only on state law issues. Therefore, Christ argued, there was no federal law question for the Supreme Court to decide.

The Supreme Court also generally hears cases where there is a conflict in decisions among the circuit courts of appeals. Again, Christ argued that there was no conflict in this case because it was decided based on the Oregon constitution while other cases that upheld random drug testing were decided based on the United States Constitution.

Another factor considered by the Supreme Court in deciding whether it will hear a particular case is whether the issue is likely to recur. Christ argued that lawsuits over random drug testing policies would not recur because they had already been decided in several other states.

The Supreme Court disagreed with the Actons' arguments. It granted Vernonia's petition and ordered the parties to file full briefs.

The Actons Respond to Vernonia's Brief

Vernonia's attorneys, Timothy R. Volpert and John A. Matterazzo of the Portland, Oregon, law firm Davis, Wright, Tremaine, filed their brief in the Supreme Court on January 12, 1995. It was now the Actons' chance to respond to the arguments made by Vernonia.

The Actons' brief first gave a history of the facts of the case. It asserted that Vernonia had overstated the drug problem in its schools. According to the Actons, the evidence of drug use in the schools consisted only of a few teachers who testified that more students were behaving badly in the late 1980s. There were mostly secondhand reports of drug use. Only one teacher testified that she had actually seen a student using drugs. The Actons agreed with the Ninth Circuit that the evidence showed only that *some* students appeared to be taking drugs.

The Actons then stated their legal arguments. First, they argued that the Fourth Amendment to the United States Constitution applies to school searches and that drug testing is a search within the meaning of the Fourth Amendment. Next, they argued that the search was unreasonable and, therefore, violated the Fourth Amendment. According to the Actons, the search was unreasonable because the school tested all athletes for drugs—not just those suspected of drug use.

Christ relied on the Supreme Court's decisions in *Skinner* and *Von Raab*. In both cases the Court upheld random drug testing of government employees. But, according to Christ, the reasons given by the Supreme Court in upholding the drug testing could not be found in the *Vernonia* case.

In *Skinner*, the Supreme Court had noted that there was a high incidence of drug use among railroad employees. This created a serious danger to the public. In *Von Raab*, the Court had noted that drug use by customs officers, who carry guns, could threaten the safety

In the *Skinner* case, the Supreme Court upheld random drug testing of railroad employees when it found a high incidence of drug use among railroad employees.

of other employees. The Supreme Court also noted that customs officers who use drugs may be tempted to take bribes from drug traffickers. Both reasons justified the government's drug testing program.

Christ also cited *New Jersey* v. *T.L.O.* He pointed out that the Supreme Court had upheld the search of a student's purse because the school official had reasonable suspicion to believe that the student had violated a school regulation.

The Actons also argued that Vernonia's drug testing policy was a substantial invasion of privacy because the student was asked to give a urine sample while a teacher stood nearby in the rest room. Under Vernonia's drug testing program, students were taken from class, escorted to the locker room, handed a specimen bottle, and instructed to fill it while the monitor waits. Adolescents, the Actons pointed out, were very self-conscious and expected to have privacy in the rest room. The Actons disagreed with Vernonia's claim that athletes have a lesser expectation of privacy.

Vernonia had argued that the school district's interest in the drug testing program was so compelling that it outweighed the students' interest in privacy; the Actons disagreed. The Actons suggested that Vernonia could use other means to achieve its goal of reducing drug use, such as educating and counseling students.

Also, the Actons pointed out, the evidence of danger to athletes was minimal. The evidence of danger caused by persons who used drugs in other areas, such as the airline and railroad industries, was far greater.

At the end of his brief, the Actons' attorney asked the Supreme Court to affirm, or uphold, the decision of the United States Court of Appeals for the Ninth Circuit. What would the Supreme Court do?

The Supreme Court still needed more information before it could decide the case of *Vernonia School District* v. *Acton.*[3] The attorneys for both sides would have to appear before the full court to present their arguments on March 28, 1995.

5

The Supreme Court Speaks

Attorneys Timothy R. Volpert and Thomas M. Christ sat in the imposing marble courtroom as the nine Justices of the United States Supreme Court took their seats to listen to oral arguments in the case of *Vernonia School District* v. *Acton*. Neither Volpert nor Christ had ever appeared before the Supreme Court. They both were excited to have the opportunity to argue in the highest court in the country, but they felt a lot of pressure to do a good job.

Volpert and Christ had a lot of support from family and friends. Volpert's wife, mother, sister, and brother-in-law had traveled from Oregon to hear the arguments. His wife, Joan, was also an appellate attorney,

Neither Timothy R. Volpert nor Thomas M. Christ had ever appeared before the Supreme Court prior to arguing the *Vernonia* case.

and she had helped him edit his brief. Also at court was a group of students from Vernonia High School. They had raised the funds they needed to fly to Washington, D.C., for this historic occasion.

Christ's family was in the audience, too. His wife, mother, father, sister, and brother anxiously awaited the arguments. Christ's father was a retired lawyer. The Actons also traveled from Oregon to hear how the Court would react to their position.

Since its inception, it has been customary during oral arguments before the Supreme Court for the Chief Justice to sit at the center of the bench. On March 28, 1995, Chief Justice William H. Rehnquist was flanked by Justices John Paul Stevens, Sandra Day O'Connor, Antonin Scalia, Anthony M. Kennedy, David Souter, Clarence Thomas, Ruth Bader Ginsburg, and Stephen Breyer. Who were these nine persons, and how would their views affect the outcome of the Vernonia School District's case?

The Chief Justice had been appointed to the bench by President Richard M. Nixon in 1971. In 1986 President Ronald Reagan nominated him for Chief Justice. Chief Justice Rehnquist was part of the so-called conservative wing of the Supreme Court. Other conservative Justices included O'Connor, Scalia, Kennedy, and Thomas. The conservatives frequently agree with the views of police officers, prosecutors, and trial judges. They do not ordinarily vote to create new rights for criminal defendants.

Justice O'Connor was the first female Supreme Court Justice, appointed by President Reagan in 1981. She had been a state senator and appellate judge in Arizona before her appointment to the Supreme Court. President Reagan also appointed Justice Scalia in 1986 and Justice Kennedy in 1988. Kennedy was known as a middle-of-the-road thinker. Justice Thomas, an African-American Republican with conservative views on affirmative action and abortion, was appointed to the United States Supreme Court by President George Bush in 1991. He replaced liberal Justice Thurgood Marshall, who retired.

Justice Stevens was appointed by President Gerald Ford in 1975. Justice Souter, who had been a state supreme court justice in New Hampshire, was appointed to the United States Supreme Court by President Bush in 1990. Justice Breyer had been a judge with the United States Court of Appeals for the First Circuit. He was appointed to the Supreme Court by President Bill Clinton in 1994. Justice Ginsburg was also appointed by President Clinton, and she became the second woman to sit on the Supreme Court. She had been a judge with the United States Court of

On March 28, 1995, the Supreme Court prepared to hear the *Vernonia* case. Justice Clarence Thomas, who replaced the retired Thurgood Marshall (shown here), was one of the Justices who would here the case.

Appeals for the District of Columbia Circuit at the time of her appointment in 1993. Justices Stevens, Souter, Breyer, and Ginsburg were more liberal in their thinking. Liberal thinkers usually favor expansive civil rights.

The United States Supreme Court begins a new term each year on the first Monday in October. Many of the cases it hears reflect political and social controversies of the time. During the 1994–1995 term, when the Supreme Court heard the *Vernonia* case, Bill Clinton was president of the United States.

As in earlier times, interesting events captured the country's attention during the mid-1990s. The O.J. Simpson trial had begun in California, and daily stories about trial strategy, the parties, the attorneys, and the presiding judge saturated newspapers, television, and radio. Political activists were fighting over affirmative action, welfare reform, and the rights of gays. Michael Jordan came out of retirement to play basketball for the Chicago Bulls, and Atlanta, Georgia, was preparing to sponsor the summer Olympics.

Arguments Begin

Despite its full agenda, on March 25, 1995, the Supreme Court turned its attention to the issues presented in *Vernonia School District* v. *Acton*. Timothy R. Volpert, representing the petitioner, the Vernonia

School District, was the first to present his arguments. Volpert began by telling the Court that hard evidence of drug use in the school district existed before the district developed its drug testing policy. He was stopped almost immediately by Justice Souter. Souter was bothered by that claim. He wanted to know what evidence the school district had other than students bragging about using drugs. Volpert replied that athletes had admitted drug use and had been arrested for it.

The Justices were concerned about how far-reaching their decision might be. Justice O'Connor asked whether the school district had tried testing students based on reasonable suspicion that a particular student might be experimenting with drugs. Volpert had to say no. Justice Kennedy then asked whether Volpert thought the Supreme Court should announce a rule that would apply only to the Vernonia School District or to all schools. Volpert said it would be reasonable for the Justices to require individual school districts to establish their own reason for drug testing. Chief Justice Rehnquist asked whether one school district could rely on findings of drug use by another school district. Volpert said they could.

What about the nonathlete school population? Should they be tested too? Volpert said, ". . . I believe

During the oral arguments, Chief Justice William Rehnquist (shown here) questioned attorney Tim Volpert on whether one school district could reasonably rely on findings of drug use by another district.

we have probably made a sufficient case for drug testing of the entire student body of the Vernonia School District."[1] What about the consent form? Was that necessary? Volpert answered more than once that the school district did not think it was necessary to have a consent form.

Justice Stevens wanted to know why the testing was confined to athletes. Volpert said the evidence at trial showed that the student body was "in a state of rebellion."[2] Justice O'Connor returned to her question about individualized suspicion. Doesn't the Fourth Amendment require individualized suspicion? The school district had taken many steps to correct the problem, Volpert argued. But he admitted again that they had not tried a drug testing program based on reasonable suspicion that a particular person was using drugs.

Justice Kennedy commented that random drug testing is less intrusive than having a teacher accuse a student of drug use. He also suggested that individualized suspicion would affect the teacher-student relationship. Volpert agreed.

The next attorney to speak was Richard H. Seamon. Seamon had filed an *amicus* brief seeking reversal on behalf of the United States. The Supreme Court allowed him a short time to present his case.

Seamon did not agree with his colleague, Volpert, that the evidence of disciplinary problems in this case would have supported drug testing for the entire student body. He argued that one of the points that made the Vernonia drug testing program reasonable was that it was confined to athletes.

Weren't athletes and their parents coerced into signing the consent form if students wanted to play sports? Seamon returned to Volpert's argument that the school district was not relying on the consent forms to justify the drug testing. He conceded, though, that it might be a type of coercion to deny students the benefits of playing sports if they did not sign the consent form.

Thomas M. Christ spoke next for the respondents, the Actons. He first challenged the school district's argument that drug testing was necessary to maintain order in the classrooms. He argued that the school did not need to test a student's urine for drugs to detect or deter disruptive behavior in class. Disruptive behavior is obvious and can be punished immediately. If the behavior is so disruptive that a teacher thinks the student's misbehavior is a result of drug use, Christ suggested, then the school could test the student.

One Justice asked, "Isn't that fraught with the risk that the teacher is going to pick out the kid he doesn't like, and those are the people that will be subject to the discipline, as opposed to the random selection?"[3] Christ argued that it was less intrusive to subject a few misbehaving students to a drug test than it was to subject every student.

What about the actual urine test? Why did Christ find it so offensive? Christ answered,

> . . . [The test] is being compelled by the government, they're watching you do it, they're taking your urine, and they're analyzing it to see what secrets lie therein, and at the same time they are compelling a student to come forward and disclose all their private medications. . . .[4]

What about a breathalyzer, the Chief Justice asked? Would Christ find that to be too intrusive? Yes, Christ asserted, for the same reason that the urine test is intrusive. The school does not need to test for alcohol levels to solve the problem of a disruptive student.

Do parents have the right to test their children for drugs? They may, Christ answered, but the schools do not have the same authority and responsibility.

The oral arguments ended one hour and two minutes after they began. Volpert found the arguments to be stimulating. Christ, on the other hand, did not think the arguments went so well for the Actons. The nine Justices retired to their chambers to consider the case.

Vernonia School District's Drug Testing Policy Upheld

After one hour of probing questions, Volpert, Christ, and Seamon had brought to a close their last chances to persuade the Supreme Court to rule in their favor. Nearly three months later, on June 26, 1995, the school district learned that the United States Supreme Court had reversed the Ninth Circuit's ruling—it had ruled in favor of the school district and upheld the drug testing policy.

How did the Supreme Court arrive at that decision? Did all of the Justices agree? What did the Court's decision mean for the rest of the country? Chief Justice Rehnquist assigned Justice Scalia to write the opinion for the Court.

Drug Testing Was a Reasonable Search Under the Fourth Amendment

All of the Justices agreed that drug testing constituted a search within the meaning of the Fourth Amendment. Remember, however, that the Fourth Amendment does not prohibit all searches; it prohibits only those that are unreasonable. The Justices were split on whether the drug testing policy adopted by the Vernonia School District was a reasonable search under the Fourth Amendment. Justices O'Connor, Stevens, and Souter concluded it was not. The majority of Justices, however, including Chief Justice Rehnquist and Justices Scalia, Kennedy, Thomas, Ginsburg, and Breyer, agreed that the drug testing policy was reasonable.

Justice Scalia wrote that the reasonableness of a search "is judged by balancing its intrusion on the individual's Fourth Amendment interests against its promotion of legitimate governmental interests."[5] Even a search that is not based on probable cause may be reasonable when special needs make probable cause impractical. Justice Scalia pointed out that the Supreme Court had found that special needs exist in public schools because of the need for teachers and administrators to keep order in the schools. He cited *New Jersey v. T.L.O.*, in which the Supreme Court ruled that a search of a student's purse was justified because a teacher suspected that a particular student had violated a school regulation.[6]

A Schoolchild's Expectation of Privacy

What type of privacy interest did schoolchildren have? Although children do not shed their constitutional rights at the schoolhouse door, the majority of Justices agreed, their rights are different in school than elsewhere. Relying on *T.L.O.*, Justice Scalia wrote that "students within the school environment have a lesser expectation of privacy than members of the population generally."[7]

What about the privacy rights of student athletes? The majority of Justices concluded that student athletes have an even lesser expectation of privacy. "School sports are not for the bashful," Justice Scalia wrote.[8] The locker rooms in Vernonia, the Supreme Court found, are typical: "no individual dressing rooms are provided; shower heads are lined up along a wall, unseparated by any sort of partition or curtain; not even all the toilet stalls have doors."[9] Also, by choosing to go out for sports, the student athlete in Vernonia must have a physical exam, keep a certain grade point average and follow certain rules of conduct.

Does obtaining a urine sample affect a student athlete's privacy interest? The Justices said no. Justice Scalia noted that in Vernonia, students remain fully clothed. Male teachers observe male students from behind, if at all. Females are in an enclosed stall, with a female monitor standing outside. Justice Scalia wrote that these conditions were nearly identical to those the student would find in a public rest room.

Justice Scalia also noted that the results of the testing are not turned over to law enforcement authorities or used for any other disciplinary hearings at the school.[10] Finally, even though students are required to list in advance what medications they may be taking, the Supreme Court had already decided in *Skinner* that was not an invasion of privacy.

The School's Interests

What interest did a public school, under the authority of the state, have in conducting drug tests? Was that interest more important than a student's interest in privacy? The majority of Justices agreed that the state's interest in deterring drug use was compelling. Justice Scalia wrote that deterring drug use by schoolchildren was at least as important as deterring drug use by engineers and railroad personnel, as the Supreme Court had decided in *Skinner*. He noted that ". . . the effects of a drug-infested school are visited not just upon the users, but upon the entire student body and faculty, as the educational process is disrupted."[11]

Justice Scalia also noted that Vernonia's program was directed to drug use by student athletes. Drugs such as cocaine, amphetamines, and marijuana could cause several serious symptoms, including high blood pressure, masking of fatigue, increased body temperature, and coronary artery spasms.

Vernonia's Policy Is Found to Be Reasonable

The Supreme Court concluded that the Vernonia School District's drug testing of athletes was reasonable under the Fourth Amendment. Justice Scalia cautioned, though, that this decision did not mean that all suspicionless drug testing would be constitutional. He noted the findings of District Court Judge Marsh that suggested that the Vernonia student body was in a state of rebellion that was being fueled by alcohol and drug abuse. The public school system, Justice Scalia wrote, "as guardian and tutor of children entrusted to its care," had developed a program to meet its responsibilities to the students. That is what made this particular program constitutional. Justice Ginsburg also noted in a separately written concurring opinion that the Supreme Court's decision did not necessarily mean that a school could require drug testing of not only its athletes but *all* of its students.

The Dissenting Opinion

Justices O'Connor, Stevens, and Souter did not agree with the majority. Justice O'Connor wrote a separate dissenting opinion expressing her views.

O'Connor noted that since 1925 the Supreme Court had ruled that blanket, suspicionless searches are unreasonable and a violation of the Fourth Amendment. The Court had allowed suspicionless searches only in limited cases where the state or federal government's interests were more important than a

Justice Sandra Day O'Connor (shown here) sided with Justices Stevens and Souter in disagreeing with the majority decision in *Vernonia*. Justice O'Connor wrote a separate dissenting opinion expressing her views.

person's privacy interests. In those cases, Justice O'Connor wrote, it was not effective to require the governmental authority to have suspicion about a particular person. In the *Vernonia* case, however, the evidence at trial showed that teachers did have firsthand knowledge of drug use by students; teachers and coaches testified that they saw students smoking marijuana and that some students admitted to using drugs. Certainly, Justice O'Connor wrote, school authorities had the means to do suspicion-based drug testing rather than blanket drug testing.

Justice O'Connor quoted the trial testimony of James Acton's father: "[Suspicionless testing] sends a message to children that are trying to be responsible citizens. . . . That they have to prove that they're innocent . . ., and I think that kind of sets a bad tone for citizenship."[12] She also noted that there was no testimony of any drug problems at Washington Grade School, where James Acton was enrolled. All of the teachers and coaches who testified at trial were employed at the high school.

Justice O'Connor concluded that it would have been far more reasonable for the school district to focus its drug testing on those students who were disrupting class. She found the majority's decision in this case "sweeps too broadly" in allowing suspicionless drug testing of all student athletes.[13]

The Reactions

Obviously, Timothy R. Volpert was pleased with the Supreme Court's decision. He had won his case on behalf of the Vernonia School District. The case was covered extensively in newspapers and on television.

Thomas M. Christ, however, was disappointed in the decision. He felt that it further eroded an individual's right to privacy under the Fourth Amendment. If children are denied the right to privacy throughout their school years, Christ believed, society could not expect them to respect the rights of others once they become adults.[14]

Legal scholars had been remarking since the days of *New Jersey* v. *T.L.O.* that the Supreme Court was weakening the guarantees of the Fourth Amendment. Would the Supreme Court change its mind about drug testing in public schools, or would *Vernonia School District* v. *Acton* remain good law?

6

The Future of School Searches

The Supreme Court's decisions in *Vernonia School District* v. *Acton* and *New Jersey* v. *T.L.O.* settled many of the nagging questions that public schools around the country had tried to resolve for many decades. The decisions finally carved out the legal standards regarding public-school officials conducting searches of students.

In *T.L.O.*, school officials were given the authority to conduct searches of student property if they had reasonable suspicion that a particular student had committed a crime or violated a school regulation. In *Vernonia*, the Supreme Court said that public-school officials could have a drug testing program if the school could show that there was a drug problem among the students. Under this scenario, the school did not need to suspect individual students to justify drug testing an entire group. In *Vernonia*, the group was student athletes.

How would these two cases hold up? Would additional changes in the school environment test the strength of the two landmark decisions?

Violence in the Schools

Lawyers presenting briefs in *New Jersey* v. *T.L.O* had alerted the Supreme Court to some shocking statistics—violence in the schools was increasing. According to the *amicus curiae* brief filed by the National School Boards Association, citing a 1978 study, "nearly three million school children may be the victims of crime each month."[1] Justice Byron White noted in the 1985 *T.L.O.* decision that "in recent years, school disorder has often taken particularly ugly forms: drug use and violent crime in the schools have become major social problems."[2] In 1985 the only question before the Supreme Court, however, was whether and under what standard a public-school official, acting alone, could legally search a particular student's personal property.

During the decade following *T.L.O.*, violence and

drug use escalated in the schools. School officials grappled with how to protect their students and maintain order on school property. Possession of guns, knives, and drugs by some students threatened the school environment. How would school officials cope with these changes? Would individual searches by public-school officials be adequate to protect students? How would advances in technology change the way searches are conducted? Would new search methods be upheld by the courts?

In the mid-1990s a high school in Philadelphia, Pennsylvania, installed a metal detector to scan student property. As students entered the school, they were led to the gymnasium and required to empty their pockets and give up their jackets and bags. The metal detector then scanned their property. One student, whose initials are F. B., emptied his pockets and surrendered a pocket knife. School officials escorted him to a holding room, and police charged him with possession of a weapon on school property. F. B. challenged the search in court.

In one of the first reported metal detector cases, the Pennsylvania court upheld the search as "reasonable" even though school officials had no individualized suspicion that F. B. was armed.[3] The court concluded that "the search was justified at its inception because of the high rate of violence in the Philadelphia public schools."[4]

Courts in Illinois and Florida followed the decision in the Pennsylvania case. In Chicago, Fenger High School sought the assistance of the local police department to conduct metal detector searches at the school.[5] When student Serrick Pruitt passed through the detector, it registered a positive reading. A police officer patted him down and found a .38-caliber revolver in his pants pocket.

Pruitt challenged the search, arguing that it was invalid because he did not consent to it. The Illinois court disagreed. The court followed the reasoning of *New Jersey* v. *T.L.O.* and tried to strike a balance between Pruitt's expectation of privacy and the school's need to maintain a safe learning environment. The court first recognized that "[j]udges cannot ignore what everybody else knows: violence and the threat of violence are present in the public schools. The situation has worsened. . . . School children are harming each other with regularity."[6] The court then found that the purpose of the metal detector screening was to protect the school for all students and not to investigate a particular crime. All students were required to walk through the detectors, and the intrusion was minimal. No student was touched by an officer unless the detector reacted. Once the metal detector reacted, the court held, a frisk search was justified.

Florida courts followed in the mid-1990s. The Dade County School Board had adopted a policy allowing random searches of students, using metal detector wands. At the time, metal detector searches were routine and constitutional in places like airports and courthouses. In the Dade County schools the Board of Education hired an independent security team to conduct random searches in randomly selected areas of each school. The search team, accompanied by a school administrator, would enter a classroom and ask the students to empty their pockets. The team would then scan the students with the metal detector wand. If the wand reacted, the security officer would pat down the student or look inside the student's property, such as a purse or book bag. Students were allowed to refuse to be searched, but refusal could subject them to some type of disciplinary action. If the search team discovered illegal drugs or weapons, the school notified police officers and students could be arrested.

After this policy came into effect, a student with the initials J. A. was arrested in a Florida public high school. As the search team entered J. A.'s classroom, the assistant principal watched as someone passed a jacket to the back of the room. One of the students placed the jacket on a shelf. A security team member took the jacket from the shelf and scanned it. He discovered a gun inside the jacket. The team found out that J. A. owned the jacket.

Citing the Illinois court's decision in *People* v. *Pruitt*, the Florida court upheld the search of J. A.'s jacket. The Florida court, too, recognized how violence had escalated in its schools: "The incidences of violence in our schools have reached alarming proportions. In the year prior to the board's implementation of the search policy, Dade County Public Schools reported both homicides and aggravated batteries as well as the confiscation from students of a very high number of weapons, including handguns."[7] Balancing the students' privacy, the type of search, and the need for the search, the court ruled that the search of J. A.'s jacket was both reasonable and constitutional.

Drug Problems in Schools

Violence was not the only problem escalating in schools. Drug use was also on the rise. In the *Vernonia* decision, Justice Scalia wrote about how devastating drugs could be to schoolchildren. He quoted from a published article on the subject:

> Maturing nervous systems are more critically impaired by intoxicants than mature ones are; childhood losses

in learning are lifelong and profound. . . . Children grow more chemically dependent more quickly than adults, and their record of recovery is depressingly poor.[8]

How would the *Vernonia* decision fare in other schools experiencing drug problems among their students?

In 1996, one year after the *Vernonia* decision, a Louisiana state appellate court upheld random searches of student property for drugs in a public school.[9] Classrooms were randomly selected by the principal for searches. Students were asked to remove all property from their pockets and place it on their desks. Then, a police officer and a trained dog entered the classroom. The dog sniffed the classroom and the student's belongings for signs of drugs. The Louisiana appellate court relied on the *Vernonia* decision to justify this type of random search because the school district had shown that there was an escalating drug problem in the schools.

Two years later, in 1998, another case almost identical to Vernonia reached a federal court of appeals. The United States Court of Appeals for the Seventh Circuit ruled in *Todd, et al.* v. *Rush County Schools* that random urine testing of students did not violate the Fourth Amendment.[10] There were two main differences between the *Vernonia* and *Todd* cases, though. First, the

Rush County drug testing program prohibited all high school students from participating in *any* extracurricular activity or driving to and from school unless the student and his or her parent consented to a random urinalysis. Extracurricular activities included athletic teams, student council, foreign language clubs, Fellowship of Christian Athletes, Future Farmers of America, and the library club. Second, the urine test did not only test for drugs; it also tested for alcohol and tobacco.

The Seventh Circuit found that Rush County's program was a reasonable means of deterring use of drugs, alcohol, and tobacco. All of these substances may affect a student's mental and physical condition, the appellate court wrote. Also, the appellate court concluded, "successful extracurricular activities require healthy students."[11]

The future of searches by public school officials is still developing. It appears from the cases decided since *New Jersey* v. *T.L.O.* that the Supreme Court is inclined to allow searches that involve a slight intrusion on the student's privacy if the state has a compelling interest in conducting the search. Recent state case law indicates that schools are becoming more and more concerned about drugs and violence, and those concerns will justify certain searches. With the development of more advanced technology, however, how intrusive will

The Supreme Court's decision on searches by public-school officials seems to indicate that the Court will allow searches that slightly intrude on students' privacy, *if* the state has a good reason to conduct the search.

searches become? Will metal detectors and drug testing still be constitutional if studies show a substantial decline in violence and drug usage by students? If drugs and violence continue to escalate, will courts permit more intrusive searches? The future holds many interesting issues for schools, students, state courts, and, undoubtedly, the Supreme Court.

Questions for Discussion

1. Discuss your thoughts on the outcome of the Supreme Court's decision in *Vernonia School District* v. *Acton.* Do you think the Supreme Court's reasoning was sound? Do you think the *Vernonia* decision overextended the Court's ruling in *New Jersey* v. *T.L.O.*? Can you see any problems with the Supreme Court's decisions in either case?

2. Pretend you are the principal of your school. Using your own school as an example, discuss what arguments you would make to the Supreme Court to convince it to uphold a random drug testing program for student athletes. Discuss what arguments you would make to uphold a random drug testing program for all students who participate in *any* extracurricular activity. What arguments would you make as a student?

3. You are the vice principal of Everytown High School. You are walking down the hall while students are changing classes, and you see two students fighting. You see one student with what appears to be a metal object in her hand. By the time you push through the crowd to reach the students, you no longer see the metal object. Do you have reasonable suspicion of either criminal activity or a violation of a school regulation to search the student? If

you believe you have reasonable suspicion, can you search the student's locker? Her purse? Her jacket?

4. Discuss the difference between probable cause and reasonable suspicion. Give examples of when a police officer might have probable cause and when a public-school official might have reasonable suspicion to justify a search.

5. You are the principal of a private high school. You have just seen a student smoking a cigarette in violation of a school regulation. The school regulation does not prevent a student from possessing cigarettes, only the smoking of cigarettes in certain areas. You want to search the student's duffel bag. What do you tell the student when he says that searching his duffel bag would be a violation of his Fourth Amendment right to privacy?

6. It is the year 2050. Violence in public schools is at an all-time high. The schools now want to strip-search all students as they enter school in the morning. You are an attorney in the public defender service. What arguments will you make opposing this new rule? What arguments would you make if you were a prosecutor?

7. It is the year 2015. Statistics show that drug use by schoolchildren has decreased substantially since the 1990s. Your school still uses random drug testing to detect drug use. How would you use recent statistics to challenge these searches? Could you make the same arguments if statistics show that disciplinary problems have substantially decreased among students?

Chapter Notes

Chapter 1. The School District's Drug Testing Policy

1. Exhibit A to Complaint for Declaratory and Injunctive Relief, *Acton* v. *Vernonia School District 47J*, Civil No. 91-1154MA, as included in Record No. 94-590 of the Supreme Court of the United States.

2. Ibid.

Chapter 2. The History of Search and Seizure Law

1. Samuel Adams, *The Writings of Samuel Adams*, vol. 2, (H. A. Cushing, 1906), pp. 350–369.

2. Ibid.

3. Fourth Amendment to the Constitution of the United States.

4. *Boyd* v. *United States*, 116 U.S. 616 (1886).

5. *Weeks* v. *United States*, 232 U.S. 383 (1914).

6. *Marron* v. *United States*, 275 U.S. 192 (1927).

7. *Carroll* v. *United States*, 267 U.S. 132, 147 (1925).

8. *Terry* v. *Ohio*, 392 U.S. 1 (1968).

9. Ibid., pp. 21, 30.

10. *Michigan* v. *Long*, 463 U.S. 1032 (1983).

11. *Boyd* v. *United States*, 116 U.S. 616 (1886).

12. Fourth Amendment to the Constitution of the United States.

13. *Wolf* v. *Colorado*, 338 U.S. 25 (1949).

14. Fourteenth Amendment to the Constitution of the United States.

15. *Mapp* v. *Ohio*, 367 U.S. 643 (1961).

16. *D.R.C.* v. *State*, 646 P.2d 252 (Alaska App. 1982); *In re Gault*, 11 Cal.App.3d 1193, 90 Cal. Rptr. 361 (1970); *In re Donaldson*, 269 Cal.App.2d 509, 75 Cal.Rptr. 220 (1969); *R.C.M.* v. *State*, 660 S.W.2d 552 (Tex.App. 1983).

17. Eugene Ehrlich, *Amo, Amas, Amat and More,* 1st ed. (New York: Harper & Row, 1985), p. 79.

18. Brief for the United States as *amicus curiae* supporting reversal, p. 18, as included in Record No. 83-712 of the Supreme Court of the United States (quoting 1 W. Blackstone, *Commentaries* 453).

19. *State* v. *Mora,* 307 So.2d 317 (La.), vacated, 423 U.S. 809 (1975), *on remand,* 330 So.2d 900 (La. 1976).

20. *Bellnier* v. *Lund,* 438 F.Supp. 47 (N.D.N.Y 1977); *State* v. *Baccino,* 282 A.2d 869 (Del.Super. 1971); *State* v. *D.T.W.,* 425 So.2d 1383 (Fla.App. 1983); *In re J.A.,* 85 Ill.App.3d 567 (1980); *People* v. *Ward,* 62 Mich.App. 46 (1975); *Doe* v. *State,* 88 N.M. 347 (1975); *People* v. *D,* 34 N.Y.2d 483 (1974); *State* v. *McKinnon,* 88 Wash.2d 75 (1977); *In re L.L.,* 90 Wis.2d 585 (1979).

21. *Board of Education* v. *Barnette,* 319 U.S. 624 (1943).

22. *Tinker* v. *Des Moines School District,* 393 U.S. 503 (1969).

23. Ibid., p. 511.

24. Ibid., p. 513.

25. Ibid., p. 514.

26. Ibid., p. 522.

27. Ibid., pp. 523–524.

28. Ibid., pp. 525–526.

29. *Goss* v. *Lopez,* 419 U.S. 565 (1975).

30. *Ingraham* v. *Wright,* 430 U.S. 651 (1977).

31. The Eighth Amendment to the Constitution of the United States.

32. *Ingraham* v. *Wright,* 430 U.S. at 669.

33. Ibid., p. 670.

34. *Miranda* v. *Arizona,* 384 U.S. 436 (1966).

35. *New Jersey* v. *T.L.O.,* 469 U.S. 325 (1985).

36. *Skinner* v. *Railway Labor Executives' Assn.* 489 U.S. 602 (1989).

37. *Treasury Employees* v. *Von Raab,* 489 U.S. 656 (1989).

38. *Michigan Dept. of State Police* v. *Sitz,* 496 U.S. 444 (1990).

Chapter 3. The Case for the Vernonia School District

1. Trial transcripts of petitioner's trial in the United States District Court for the District of Oregon, p. 20, as included in Record No. 94-590 of the Supreme Court of the United States.

2. Ibid., p. 21.

3. Ibid., p. 22.

4. Ibid., p. 46.

5. *Acton* v. *Vernonia School District 47J,* 796 F.Supp. 1354 (D.Or. 1992).

6. *Schaill* v. *Tippecanoe County School District,* 864 F.2d 1309 (7th Cir. 1988).

7. *Derdeyn* v. *University of Colorado,* 832 P.2d 1031 (Colo.App. 1991).

8. *Hill* v. *NCAA,* 7 Cal.App.4th 1738, 273 Cal.Rptr. 402, *petition for review granted* 276 Cal.Rptr. 319, 801 P.2d 1070 (1990); *Brooks* v. *East Chambers Consol. Ind. School Dist.,* 730 F.Supp. 759 (S.D.Tex. 1989), *aff'd* 930 F.2d 915 (5th Cir. 1991); *Anable* v. *Ford,* 653 F.Supp. 22, *modified in part,* 663 F.Supp. 149 (W.D.Ark. 1985).

9. *Acton* v. *Vernonia School District 47J,* 23 F.3d 1514 (9th Cir. 1994).

10. Eugene Ehrlich, *Amo, Amas, Amat, and More,* 1st ed. (New York: Harper & Row, 1985), p. 79.

11. Ibid.

12. Petition for writ of *certiorari,* p. 39, as included in Record No. 94-590 of the Supreme Court of the United States.

13. Ehrlich, p. 42.

Chapter 4. The Case for the Actons

1. Trial transcripts of petitioner's trial in the United States District Court for the District of Oregon, p. 17, as included in Record No. 94-590 of the Supreme Court of the United States.

2. *Acton* v. *Vernonia School District 47J,* 23 F.3d 1514 (9th Cir. 1994), attached as Appendix A, pp. 20a-21a, to petition for writ of *certiorari,* as included in Record No. 94-590 of the Supreme Court of the United States.

3. *Vernonia School District 47J* v. *Acton,* Record No. 94-590 of the Supreme Court of the United States.

Chapter 5. The Supreme Court Speaks

1. Transcript of oral arguments, p. 9, as included in Record No 94-590 of the United States Supreme Court.

2. Ibid., p. 12.

3. Ibid., p. 32.

4. Ibid., p. 48.

5. *Vernonia School District 47J* v. *Acton*, 515 U.S. 646, 652–653 (1995).

6. *New Jersey* v. *T.L.O.*, 469 U.S. 325 (1985).

7. *Vernonia*, 515 U.S. at 657, quoting *T.L.O.*, 469 U.S. at 348.

8. Ibid.

9. *Vernonia*, 515 U.S. at 657.

10. Ibid.

11. Ibid., p. 662.

12. Ibid., p. 665.

13. Ibid., p. 682.

14. Author phone interview with Thomas M. Christ, February 9, 1998.

Chapter 6. The Future of School Searches

1. Brief of the National School Boards Association, p. 10, Record No. 83-712 of the Supreme Court of the United States (citing National Institute of Education, *Violent Schools—Safe Schools: The Safe School Study Report to the Congress* 31–32 (1978)).

2. *New Jersey* v. *T.L.O.*, 469 U.S. 325, 339 (1985).

3. *In the Interest of F.B.*, 442 Pa.Super. 216, 658 A.2d 1378 (1995).

4. Ibid., p. 1382.

5. *People* v. *Pruitt*, 662 N.E.2d 540 (Ill.App. 1 Dist. 1996).

6. Ibid., p. 546.

7. *State* v. *J.A.*, 679 So.2d 316, 320 (Fla.App. 3 Dist. 1996).

8. *Vernonia School District 47J* v. *Acton*, 515 U.S. 646, 661 (1995), quoting Hawley, *The Bumpy Road to Drug-Free Schools*, 72 Phi Delta Kappan 310, 314 (1990).

9. *State* v. *Barrett*, 683 So.2d 331 (La.Ct.App. 1996).

10. *Todd, et al.*, v. *Rush County Schools*, 1998 U.S.App. LEXIS 372 (7th Cir. 1998).

11. Ibid.

Glossary

amici curiae **briefs**—Briefs filed by individuals or organizations (such as the ACLU) who are not a party to the case but who have an interest in its outcome. *Amici curiae* is a Latin term meaning "friends of the court."

brief—A legal document stating the facts and legal theories of a party's case.

dissenting opinion—A written opinion by those Justices who disagree with the majority opinion.

due process—A legal concept that establishes procedures to ensure an individual's rights and liberties in all legal proceedings.

evidence—Information consisting of testimony of witnesses, documents, or tangible objects that tend to prove the prosecutor's or defense attorney's case. The judge presiding over the trial determines whether the evidence is admissible, that is, whether the jury will be allowed to hear or see the evidence. Evidence can be either direct or circumstantial.

exclusionary rule—A rule of law providing that in certain circumstances unlawfully seized evidence, that is, evidence that is seized in violation of an individual's Fourth

Amendment right against unreasonable searches and seizures, is inadmissible in state or federal criminal trials.

grand jury—A group of citizens summoned by the government to hear the testimony of witnesses and examine evidence in order to determine whether there is probable cause to believe a crime has been committed and that the suspect is the person who committed the crime.

incorporation doctrine—A legal theory used by the United States Supreme Court to apply the Bill of Rights to the states through the Due Process Clause of the Fourteenth Amendment.

independent source doctrine—A legal concept providing that evidence that is discovered wholly independent from unlawful police conduct is admissible at trial.

inevitable discovery rule—A legal concept providing that unlawfully seized evidence is admissible at trial if the evidence would inevitably have been discovered by lawful means.

motion—A legal document asking the court to rule on a particular legal issue. For example, a motion to suppress evidence is a request for the court to find that evidence seized by police is not admissible at trial because it was seized in violation of the defendant's constitutional rights.

petition for writ of *certiorari*—A legal document that must be filed by a person who wants the United States Supreme Court to hear his or her case.

probable cause—Sufficient reason, based on existing facts and circumstances, to believe that a crime has been committed or that a certain person committed the crime, or that property is evidence of the crime. Probable cause is a required element for some legal searches and seizures.

prosecutor—An attorney, also known as a district attorney or a United States attorney, who represents the state or federal government in criminal proceedings.

warrant—A legal document authorizing a law enforcement official to take some action. For example, a search warrant authorizes a law enforcement official to search for particular items; an arrest warrant authorizes the arrest of a suspect. To obtain a search warrant, a judge or magistrate must find that law enforcement officials applying for the warrant have probable cause to believe that the thing or place to be searched contains evidence of a crime. To obtain an arrest warrant, a judge or magistrate must find that law enforcement officials applying for the warrant have probable cause to believe that the person to be arrested committed a crime.

Further Reading

Alderman, Ellen, and Caroline Kennedy. *The Right to Privacy.* New York: Alfred A. Knopf, Inc., 1995.

David, Andrew. *Famous Supreme Court Cases.* Minneapolis, Minn.: Lerner, 1980.

Habenstreit, Barbara. *Changing America and the Supreme Court.* New York: Julian Messner, 1970.

Jenkins, George H. *American Government: The Constitution.* Vero Beach, Fla.: Rourke, 1990.

Lewis, Anthony. *Gideon's Trumpet.* New York: Random House, 1964.

Lowe, William. Human Rights: *Blessings of Liberty: Safeguarding Civil Rights.* Vero Beach, Fla.: Rourke, 1992.

Rehnquist, William H. *The Supreme Court—How It Was, How It Is.* New York: William Morrow, 1987.

Ritchie, Donald A. *Know Your Government: The U.S. Constitution.* New York: Chelsea House, 1989.

Sexton, John, and Nat Brandt. *How Free Are We? What the Constitution Says We Can and Cannot Do.* New York: M. Evans, 1986.

Internet Addresses

K9 Academy for Law Enforcement: Case Law Center
<http://www.policek9.com/lawnarc.htm>

United States Supreme Court Cases: Listing
<http://oyez.nwu.edu/cases/cases.cgi>

Index